1000 STORIES
AND ILLUSTRATIONS
FOR ALL OCCASIONS

Prochnow Speaker's Library

1800 Quips and Illustrations for All Occasions
700 Illustrations and Ideas for Speakers
400 Illustrations for Ministers and Teachers
1000 Stories and Illustrations for All Occasions
1400 Ideas for Speakers and Toastmasters

Michael Angelo Angelo

1000 Stories
and Illustrations
for All Occasions

Herbert V. Prochnow

BakerBooks
A Division of Baker Book House Co
Grand Rapids, Michigan 49516

© 1972 by Herbert V. Prochnow

Reprinted 1973, 1994 by Baker Books
a division of Baker Book House Company
P.O. Box 6287, Grand Rapids, MI 49516-6287

Previously published as *The Speaker's and Toastmaster's Handbook*
and as *1000 Quips, Stories, and Illustrations for All Occasions*

Printed in the United States of America

ISBN 0-8010-7144-5

CONTENTS

Chapter 7

Chapter 8

PREFACE

With more than 1,000 witticisms, humorous stories, biographical illustrations, ideas for speeches and sermons, and material for special events, this book can be helpful on many occasions.

These hundreds of items can be used to create interest in speeches, add sparkle to introductions by toastmasters, and stimulate conversation. They may provide humor and help to clarify and emphasize a point in a speech so it will be remembered. They may also provide inspiration.

This reference book can be useful not only to the chairman or toastmaster at a special event, such as a luncheon or dinner, but the witticisms included may also be used, for example, to enliven a dull committee meeting and make it more interesting.

One chapter contains scores of items for special occasions such as Christmas, New Year's Day, Mother's Day, Fourth of July, Thanksgiving and other significant days.

There are also examples of introductions which toastmasters have used and illustrations also of how speakers have opened and closed addresses.

It is hoped that the use of this practical reference material will assist the reader both in the preparation of speeches and in stressing major points in an address.

A witticism, a humorous story or a good illustration may make a significant contribution to the effectiveness of a speech, or may even relieve a tense moment in a discussion.

To the extent that this book makes speeches and conversation more interesting, it will have served a useful purpose.

—Herbert V. Prochnow

CHAPTER 1

WITTICISMS FOR TOASTMASTERS AND SPEAKERS

We use more oil than any other nation, but after all we have more troubled waters.

When you look at the condition of the world, you have a suspicion that an efficiency expert must be in charge.

Modern marketing is wonderful. You can get indigestion and a remedy for it at the same store.

You never know how lucky you are until you go into a gift store and see all the things your friends haven't sent you.

You can live much longer if you quit everything that makes you want to.

Business is normal when consumers earn $30 a day and spend $40.

The first thing a young man wants when he gets a little money is a car and the first thing he wants when he gets a car is a little money.

You sometimes wonder whether the government machinery in the Middle East wouldn't run better with a little less oil.

Old age is that period in life when you finally learn that you are not the center of the universe.

Most of us get so little exercise that the only time our muscles ripple is when the wind blows.

If you dodge cars, you are a pedestrian. If you dodge responsibility, you are a politician running for office.

The world is changing so rapidly that we no longer live and learn. We live and unlearn.

The more things change, the more they are the same. The old dime novel now sells for $7.95.

Memory is a great asset. It is the only thing that stands between the world and a nuclear war.

One trouble with life is that industry takes so much more effort than ambition.

All men are born free and equal but many of them grow up and get married.

We suggest that before management-labor wage settlements are made, the people be asked how much they would like to be soaked.

A wise man soon learns that silence cannot be misquoted.

Microphones relieve the strain on the speaker's voice but what we need is a device that relieves the strain on the listener's intelligence.

What keeps this world going is that we want more than we need.

The man who says our wildlife is disappearing has apparently never heard about juvenile crime.

One of the reasons King Solomon got a reputation for wisdom was that he never had to run a foreign aid program.

With the shortage of parking space, what this country needs is a small portable automobile.

What this country needs is a statesman who can expand welfare programs without soaking the taxpayer.

A man who stole $4.20 got 90 days. We have our faults, but we don't like a piker.

A recent story on the big new rich in this country proves again that all work and no play makes jack.

It's pretty hard to tell where some politicians stand while they are running hard for the next election.

We are waiting for the day when the big cities clean up crime the way crime cleans up the big cities.

Business continues on the upswing and so do prices.

No one is more disappointed than the fellow who gets what he has coming to him.

You never get too old to learn something foolish and do something stupid.

Money is what you spend for luxuries and owe for necessities.

Advice—The cheapest commodity. The supply is great and the demand is small.

A fisherman always catches his biggest fish by the tale.

If the nations heed not Sinai, how can we expect them to listen to Washington, D.C.?

"Rice," says an authority, "requires more moisture than any other cereal." How about wild oats?

All nations have rights, except of course the small ones.

The two principal kinds of time for a woman are standard and her wristwatch.

A doctor says the American people are becoming round-shouldered. Probably one of the results of the tax load.

One of these days maybe the government will take all our income and then let some of it be withheld each week for us.

Is it loose management of the economy that gives us tight money?

"It's me" and "He don't" are wrong, but sometimes we think they ain't.

A spaceman from Mars could easily pick out the most civilized nations here. They are the only ones who know how to make atom bombs.

When a businessman considers the amount of paper that passes over his desk, he may decide that next to a dog a wastebasket is man's best friend.

Nature is wonderful—she makes us imperfect, but blind to our faults.

Some day we hope the do-it-yourself idea will include thinking.

These are the good old days you will look back to in 1995.

What the world needs is six months of peace so we can catch up on our worrying.

Some persons are already working a 30-hour week but they spend 40 doing it.

The doctors say if you quit everything that makes you want to live longer you will.

We would all be in favor of progress if it didn't involve so much change.

If you wear out the eraser before you use up the pencil, you are making too many errors.

An argument is a question with two sides and no end.

We never understood why "economy" means the large size in toothpaste but the small size in cars.

It's remarkable what a good pencil can do for a golf score.

Style is something that goes in one era and out the other.

Nothing turns attention your way in an office like a mistake.

One thing you have to say about ignorance is that it causes a lot of interesting arguments.

Money still talks, but sometimes you have to increase the volume to get the message through.

A pessimist is a person who can't understand why he doesn't feel bad when he feels good.

Middle age is when it takes you longer to rest up than it does to get tired.

A bowler is a person who is so quiet he can hear a pin drop.

It isn't easy now to find a wife who will help her husband with the housework.

No tool beats a checkbook in finishing a do-it-yourself job.

A vacation is when you borrow money to live beyond your means for two weeks.

The fact that there is no fool like an old fool proves what experience can do for you.

Empires rise and fall but prices only rise.

A wife is a great comfort during all those troubles a bachelor never has.

Remember way back when girls had such names as Patience and Prudence.

The crossword puzzle dates back to 2000 B.C., which accounts for the obsolete words in most modern ones.

If the meek inherit the earth, they will inherit debt enough to keep them that way.

In the old days parents used to kiss their children good night at bedtime, but now they can't wait up that late.

A relative is someone who wonders how you manage to get by.

That tall Tower of Babel was probably the first United Nations.

God made the country but it was man who put the mortgages and installment payments on it.

With present prices every house is a house that Jack built.

The fellow who asks whether women are really willing to assume places of authority obviously isn't married.

A southern resort is a place where the palms are both perpendicular and horizontal.

The only bit of humor we get from Soviet Russia is an occasional claim that it has been insulted.

The pictures painted by Picasso are nothing compared to those painted by a good real estate agent.

The three R's of education at some colleges—Rah, Rah, Rah!

Of course the country is prosperous. We have twice as much money and it buys half as much.

Man's inhumanity to man makes millions go through the yellow light.

The large number of Volkswagens in this country seem to be an example of Hans across the sea.

Every husband knows that the old joke about a woman shopping all day long and buying nothing is a joke.

We only eat oysters in a month with an "R" and snails in a month with a "Z."

What would you do first if you were given a million dollars? If you are smart, you would count it.

A sea monster is discovered in a Scottish lake each year. It can't be a government project because it moves.

A convict studied law in prison and got himself out, which we presume shows the value of good vocational guidance.

The chaplains who pray daily for the United States Senate and the House might say a word occasionally for the taxpayer.

It's hard to distinguish between the person who didn't know the gun was loaded and the driver who didn't know he was.

Life insurance sales are up, which seems to indicate life is so merry that people figure it can't last long.

A pessimist is a person who has been able to tell whether the public is light-hearted or light-headed.

You need to start worrying about your health if you can't sleep when it's time to get up.

With new school houses having glass walls the kids can see the fire engine go by without standing up.

In Latin America a political party is a man with a good voice, a large vocabulary, and a microphone.

You can't fool all the people all the time but someone is always trying it.

Even after Congress finally adjourns there will probably still be some things wrong with the country.

It's a good thing for youth to have its day because it will age rapidly when the taxpaying begins.

A successful American novelist never went beyond high school which apparently is one requirement for writing modern novels.

The person who says he welcomes criticism ought to be happy most of the time.

If Little Bo-Peep lost her sheep today, the government would pay her for not finding them.

The mail service may be slower than it used to be, but its still fast enough when you see what you get.

About the time the underdeveloped nations cut down their death rates from diseases, they will get highways and automobiles.

Someone has said mankind will never achieve anything more terrible than nuclear bombs. However, we have a little more faith in civilization.

Good government pays. The other kind does, too, but not the same people.

The fellow who never went to college has one advantage. He isn't filled with gloom on Saturdays when the football team loses.

With all the college scholastic rules now, it's almost impossible for an amateur to make a decent living in any sport.

A new novel is described by critics as sincere, refreshing and clean which will just about wreck its sales.

We suppose the ruins of ancient Egypt only prove that ancient Egyptian wives had a shot at backing the chariot into the garage.

The position of woman in relation to man in Soviet Russia is not good, as she is only his equal over there.

An American who visited Moscow recently was placed on an outgoing plane one hour after his arrival. His new book "Soviet Russia From the Inside" will be published shortly.

A vacation is when you spend two weeks you have and the money you borrow for a brief experience of living higher than you can afford.

It doesn't pay to lock the barn door after the horse is stolen if you can open a summer theatre.

Year-in and year-out, probably the steadiest job in Washington is building pigeon holes for "must" legislation.

France is taking hard measures to stop sharply rising prices. Apparently 50 million Frenchmen can't be wrung.

Nothing is as successful as a motor cycle cop selling tickets for the policemen's ball.

An American is a person who believes in the absolute necessity of balancing the budget in good times, but puts it off with the expectation that a miracle will come along and do the trick.

Good breeding consists in concealing how much we think of ourselves and how little we think of other people.

The best things in life are free. It's the worst things that are so expensive.

A never-failing way to get rid of a fellow is to tell him something for his own good.

In a few years there will be more than 200 million automobiles in the U.S.A. If you want to cross the street, you'd better do it now.

Comment regarding the Prime Minister of a certain country: When he isn't acting as God, he acts as Prime Minister.

Sympathy: That which one woman offers to another in exchange for all the details.

Living in the lap of luxury isn't bad except that you never know when luxury is going to stand up.

When you get a chance to buy things for a song, it's a good idea to check the accompaniment.

A crank is a man who has a different hobby than your own.

The man who attends strictly to his own business has a steady job.

Inflation is when nobody has enough money, because everybody has too much.

When you help out a man in trouble, you can be sure of one thing; he won't forget you—the next time he's in trouble.

When a speech is boiled down it isn't so dry.

A theory is a hunch with a college education.

It's costing us more to make history than the stuff is worth.

Breathes there a man with soul so dead who has not lately, sadly, said: "Can this be my own, my native land?"

Live within your income and you'll live without worry—and a lot of other things.

How well most people like hard work depends upon whether they are doing it or paying for it.

There's a new gas that puts a rabbit in your tank—it's for short hops.

Early to bed, early to rise, 'til you make enough cash to do otherwise.

Most persons will not throw away life at one time, but they will throw away some each day.

Thank goodness we live in a free country, where a man may say what he thinks—if he isn't afraid of his wife, his neighbors, or his boss, and if he's sure it won't hurt his business or his reputation.

Some people speak from experience and others, from experience, don't speak.

An old-timer is a fellow who remembers when it cost more to run a car than to park it.

If living conditions don't stop improving in this country, we're going to run out of humble beginnings for our great men.

Business is that which if you do not have enough of, you go out of.

Take it like a man—blame it on your wife.

To err is human and usually lots of fun.

Half the people in this world are miserable because they can't have what makes the other half miserable.

A skillful politician can rock the boat and then make you believe he can save you in a storm.

Three things in this world are always unexpected—triplets.

Rejecting things because they are "old-fashioned" could rule out the sun and the moon.

He who devotes sixteen hours a day to hard study may be as wise at 60 as he thought himself at 20.

Boy to Santa Claus, "This may be the last year I believe in you."

A good listener is a person who is smart enough to think about something else.

Only a collect call makes a telephone booth comfortable.

Every dog has his day but the road-hog has all Sunday afternoon.

Failure is the path of least persistence.

It's very difficult to look slick if you have too much span.

The fellow that agrees to be chairman of a committee is either naive or an insurance salesman.

Luck seems to have a peculiar attachment to work.

If you were sure you wouldn't be found out, what is it that you would like to do?

A vacation is a short period of recreation followed by a long period of recuperation.

You can get a lot of first-hand experience from a second-hand car.

What this country needs is a politician who knows what this country needs.

The fishing was so bad on our vacation that even the liars didn't catch any.

Don't complain if your dreams don't come true—neither do your nightmares.

Some persons drop a dime in a tin cup and walk away as if they had solved the nation's unemployment problem.

Just keep smiling and everyone will wonder what you have been up to.

A committee is a group of three persons—one to do the work and the other two to pat him on the back or criticize.

The modern girl may have her little weaknesses, but she isn't effeminate.

A doctor says you are what you eat, and in that case we are a bad egg this morning.

It is very difficult for a young couple to learn that other people have perfect children too.

Most of us have enough character to say "No" to temptation once weakly.

Nobody appreciates the beauty of Autumn more than the fellow who has no leaves to rake.

Happiness is when you are too busy to know you are miserable.

We don't like people who won't admit their faults, because we would if we had any.

If a person didn't have experience, how could he recognize a mistake when he makes it again?

A diplomat is a person who thinks twice before saying nothing, whereas a politician says nothing without thinking.

An old-timer is a person who remembers when people rested on Sunday instead of Monday.

If you want people to like you, listen carefully to a lot of things you already know.

The thing we admire about the hero in the Westerns is his ability to keep his shirt clean through all that riding and fighting.

The cost of driving a car still isn't high enough to relieve the congestion in the hospital emergency wards.

Even the state of matrimony can't endure half slave and half free.

Always tell your wife everything—especially before someone else does.

Why is it that it is always the politicians and not the people who know what they want?

When the French hotel clerk asked the tourist whether he was a foreigner, the tourist said, "No sir, American."

We expect to hear next that the Treasury has abolished the $5.00 bill because the $10.00 bill has taken its place.

There are 5,000 different languages in the world and money and credit cards speak all 5,000 of them.

Three burglars entered a night club and escaped without losing anything.

The annual race between weeds and vegetables is under way and the results are the same as usual.

One hears very little about the high cost of golf balls.

Although prosperity has lasted a long time, we imagine quite a few families still have things that aren't mortgaged yet.

A telephone expert says Americans waste millions of minutes a day saying, "Hello." In a family of teen-agers even more time is wasted just waiting for a chance to say, "Hello."

An optimist is a person who thinks he will never be a sucker again.

Most cocktail parties sound like feeding time at the zoo.

Why is it that a politician never seems so wise in Congress as he seems stumping for office?

We pay taxes to support bureaucrats to see that we pay taxes to support bureaucrats.

Love may be blind, but it doesn't stay that way long.

One good way to learn how to think fast on your feet is to be a pedestrian.

A political candidate may not be sound, but he makes a lot of it, anyhow.

Soviet Russia is hard hit by low agricultural production, but what does she expect with one half her male population over here dancing in ballets?

Nature didn't make us perfect, but she made us blind to our faults.

The reason foreigners find English so difficult is that they try to speak it correctly.

You may out-bluff the other driver, but will you outlive him?

One of life's briefest moments is the time between reading the sign on the expressway and realizing you just missed the exit ramp.

As you grow older, you start to think, and bingo! First thing you know you're sound asleep!

The trouble with what melts in your mouth is the way it bulges in front of the mirror.

To do a great and important work, two things are necessary: a plan, and not quite enough time.

Most auto accidents occur on Saturday and Sunday, proving it's a great life if you don't weekend.

All that I am or hope to be, I owe.

I don't like Junior crossing the railroad tracks. In fact, I don't like Junior.—*Groucho Marx*

Just when you're ready to give your son a share in the business you find the government has beaten him to it.

If you do not wear seat belts, be sure to wear a soft felt hat to protect your ears as your head goes through the windshield.

The man who was spurred to success by memories of his run-down hillside home of his youth isn't half so proud of his three-bedroom house in town as he is of the run-down hillside cottage he buys as a summer home and status symbol.

The best thing for newlyweds to feather their nest with is plenty of cash down.

"Opened by Mistake" applies to more mouths than letters.

In fifty years the automobile has replaced the horse as everyday transportation and the horse has replaced the automobile as a status symbol.

"Golf is a sport in which the ball usually lies poorly, but the player well."

Perfection is the bull's-eye of a target that no one has ever hit.

People limited in knowledge of a subject are often unlimited in their dissertations on it.

Those who don't know and don't know they don't know seldom agree with those who do know.

The astronaut's wife is strange in one way, beyond doubt: Her heart rejoices when she sees her husband down and out.

The average household consists of a husband who makes the money, and a wife and children who make it necessary.

Then there was the wave that grew and grew until finally it was fit to be tide.

With today's transportation, there's no such thing as a distant relative.

Matrimony is the only state that allows a woman to work eighteen hours a day.

Nothing grows faster than a fish from the time he bites until he gets away.

The ideal combination in traffic is to have horse-sense in the car equal to the horse-power under the hood.

You have to do your own growing up no matter how tall your grandpa was.

All that half the world knows about the other half of the world is that it lives beyond its income.

Many of the younger generation are alike in many disrespects.

In the old days we had one Death Valley, but now we have one between the curbs in every city.

Many Americans wish they were as rich as foreigners think they are.

We like the fellow who comes right out and says he agrees with us.

Many a boy at sixteen can't believe that some day he will be as dumb as his dad.

The clinging-vine type of woman is a thing of the past, because it is so hard to find anything solid to cling to any more.

Being told things for your own good seldom does you any.

This is a free country, and every man can do just as his wife pleases.

When you reduce, you have more to laugh about, but less to laugh with.

A danger sign on a highway can't talk, but it is not as dumb as the guy who doesn't believe it.

You can read some persons like a book, but you can't shut them as easily.

Most of us have too many days left over each month at the end of the money.

When your ship comes in, the government helps you dock it.

A man finds it about as hard to thread a needle as a woman does to drive through a 12-foot garage doorway.

It's a shame to waste a college education on a freshman who already knows everything.

The fellow who laughs at his troubles never runs out of things at which to laugh.

Poverty is not a disgrace, but it has nothing else in its favor.

What you don't know may not hurt you, but it may make you look pretty stupid.

No one is more disappointed than the person who gets what he has coming to him.

If you drive with one arm, you end up either walking up or being carried up a church aisle.

There is nothing busier than an idle rumor.

If you don't read any books, you have no advantage over the man who can't read.

A mistake is at least evidence that someone tried to do something.

When we stop to think, we don't always start up again.

The person who loses his head probably doesn't miss it.

Comfortable chairs are worn out with hard use; uncomfortable ones survive and become antiques.

Memory keeps telling you that you know the guy but can't remember his name.

The one book that always has a sad ending is the check book.

To insure the education of teen-agers, parents need to pull a few wires: TV, telephone, ignition.

Many tombstones are carved by chiseling in traffic.

Girls won't have hourglass figures if they ask for seconds.

The best way to remember your wife's birthday is to forget it once.

The most comforting thing about the top ten hits is that next week they won't be.

A fair-weather friend is one who is always around when he needs you.

Variety is the spice of life, but monotony provides the groceries.

More and more people are buying their homes on the outskirts of their incomes.

It's human to have your mind wander, but the trouble comes when you follow it.

Children are creatures who disgrace you by exhibiting in public the example you set for them at home.

The only person ever to get his work done by Friday was Robinson Crusoe.

If at first you don't succeed, you're typical.

After paying for the wedding, about the only thing a father has left to give away is the bride.

He travels faster who has the ability to fold road maps.

The university brings out all abilities including incapability.

Old-timer: One who remembers when you could promise a child the moon without having to buy him a space suit.

It's a wise father who throws away his old report cards.

If you're going around in circles, maybe you're cutting too many corners.

You don't realize you are buying goldbricks until you get the builder's estimate on your new home.

Driving's a lot like baseball—it's the number of times you get home safely that counts.

The best thing some self-made men can do is deny it.

Advertising is the fine art of making you think you have longed for something all your life that you never heard of before.

Inflation is when, after you get the money to buy something, it isn't enough.

On a certain island in the South Pacific there are no taxes, unemployment, crime, beggars, television, or inhabitants.

We've never known it to fail: When anyone offers to "tell the honest truth," he's about to say something very unpleasant.

The best things in life are free, but what a pity that the next best things are so expensive!

Any man who gives in when he is right is weak—and probably married.

Some think that the moon won't be able to support life. Well, it's not such an easy thing on this old planet either.

Sign outside an auto repair shop: "May we have the next dents, please?"

When you get a chance to buy things for a song, it's a good idea to check the accompaniment.

An optimist is a fellow who marries his secretary and thinks he can go right on dictating to her.

The trouble with punctuality is that often there's nobody there to appreciate it.

The trouble with telling little white lies is that they pick up so much dirt while traveling.

Tomorrow: one of the greatest labor-saving inventions of all time.

If money could talk, it would ask, "What happened?"

One of the latest computers is so human it blames its mistakes on others.

Lend some neighbors a garden tool, and they'll always come back for mower.

It's tough to make a mistake, but it's tougher still to find out you're so unimportant that nobody noticed it.

A kindergarten teacher is a woman who knows how to make little things count.

By the time you find out what makes the world go 'round, you're too dizzy to care.

An executive is one who never puts off until tomorrow what he can get someone else to do today.

The guy who brags that he has a head on his shoulders, sometimes has a point there.

No-hit pitcher: A ball player who can throw a ball faster than you can shake a stick at it.

An optimist is one who puts a stamp on a letter and marks it "rush."

A conference is the confusion of one man multiplied by the number present.

When father and son step out together today, the one with the beard is the son.

An old-timer is someone who remembers when people who wore jeans worked.

A marriage is a success when they live happily even after.

Some people are easily entertained. All you have to do is sit down and listen to them.

When we have to swallow our own medicine the spoon always seems too big.

A fool and his credit card are some party.

You know you've reached middle-age when it's a doctor and not a traffic cop who warns you to slow down.

Vacation is simply that period of time when you get too active and too tired on your own time.

All suburbanites are endowed with certain inalienable rights: life, liberty, and the pursuit of crabgrass.

What this country needs is a power mower that can be operated from an air-conditioned room.

In some beauty salons the talk alone can curl your hair.

If you do not know what you want, the next best thing is to learn to take what you get.

A pessimist is an optimist who voted for a politician he thought would eliminate government waste.

Modern pioneer: The mother who manages to get through a rainy Saturday with the television set out of order.

Appearances are often deceiving. A woman's thumb may have a man under it.

The unlucky man who can't forget his business on vacation is simply doomed to be a success.

A gentleman today is a man who holds the door open so his wife can carry in $25 worth of groceries in two small sacks.

A person's mind may be broad but have no depth.

An optimist is a person who thinks you can take a nice leisurely drive with the family on Saturday afternoon.

The ship of state is one vessel that seems to move best in a fog.

Some persons go to work each day, but not after they get there.

With some married couples the big difference of opinion is whether he earns too little or she spends too much.

Public opinion is simply the private opinion of one person who made enough noise to attract some converts.

We don't suppose competition in the automobile industry will end until they get to the last pedestrian.

It takes three generations to make a gentleman because most of us only work at it part time.

A boom period is one in which the consumer is well enough off to live beyond his means.

Most of the people who do astonishing things in life are alone, especially on a golf course or while fishing.

Education pays, unless you are an educator.

About all the world sees of the peace dove is the bill.

If a man has to stand on his dignity, he is very short.

It takes a very big wave of indignation to have much of a cleaning effect.

There are still quite a few American families so poor they have only one car.

One thing is certain—you never get lonely at the bottom of the ladder.

The little boy prayed that he might be made a good boy—but not until the day after tomorrow.

How soon Russia gets out of the satellite countries will have something to do with how much.

We used to dread chaos in the world, but it isn't so bad now that we are used to it.

No small boy can understand why they have grown-ups judge jam and jelly exhibits at the country fairs.

A man's achievements in business depend partly on whether he keeps his mind or his feet on the desk.

Isn't it funny that no one ever asks a man how he combines marriage and a career?

Before marriage he talks and she listens. After marriage she talks and he listens. Later they both talk and the neighbors listen.

Adolescent: One who is well informed about anything he doesn't have to study.

The older we get the farther we had to walk to school in our youth.

Travel agency sign: Please Go Away!

Sign on a reducing parlor: Come in—what have you got to lose?

While this nation still doesn't have a good five-cent cigar, it does have a good nickel quarter.

Time's a great healer, but it's no beauty specialist.

Things are pretty well evened up in this world. Other people's troubles are not as bad as yours, but their children are a lot worse.

The difference between gossip and news is whether you hear it or tell it.

Before television no one ever knew what a headache looked like.

You can tell what condition a man is in if you know what he takes two at a time—stairs or pills.

A pessimist is a fellow who really knows what's going on.

A person who is reckless in crossing busy streets may be known either as a "jay-walker" or "the deceased."

Nothing is easier to pick up and harder to drop than a prejudice.

When you feel yourself turning green with envy, you are ripe for trouble.

Do you know what Whistler said to his mother when he came home and found her scrubbing the floor? "Mother, you are off your rocker!"

Office secretary on phone: "He's out to lunch now but he won't be gone long. Nobody took him."

Genius: a man who shoots at something no one else can see, and hits it.

Every good idea must have a beginning. Maybe all of us could start living within our incomes on Monday and Friday.

Even if automobiles can't push trains off the track, they certainly keep trying.

Things are never as bad as they seem. There must be millions of Russians who don't hate anyone.

A newspaper says it's dangerous for a young man to propose while he is driving a car. It's dangerous anywhere, son.

No one has a touch that thrills you like a dentist.

When it comes to solving your problems, perspiration is the best solvent of all.

It's not always easy to get the rising generation up in the morning.

With 80 million automobiles there is no such thing any more as the man-in-the-street.

Our hero is the person who moves that the minutes of the last meeting be accepted without reading them.

Philosophy is what rich people use to convince the rest of us that it's no disgrace to be poor.

Most Americans are so restless they don't feel at home at home.

Scientists have invented an earthquake detector that goes off like an alarm clock. What is really needed is an alarm clock that goes off like an earthquake.

If the world is getting smaller, why do they keep raising postal rates?

Some people are like blisters—they don't show up until the work is done.

The first signs of Spring are the blooming idiots on the highways.

You don't have to have a remarkable memory to recall when you wished for the income you can't live on now.

Making out an income tax form is a lesson in addition, multiplication and extraction.

When you speak to other people for their good, it is influence; and when other people speak to you for your good, it is interference.

In Hollywood the man with only one ulcer is classed as a third-rate executive.

Some actors think they are elevating the stage when they are merely depressing the audience.

Nothing worries the pessimist like the optimist who says there's nothing to worry about.

There's only one thing that's keeping millions of more people from going into the stock market—the supermarket.

When a mule has it, no one calls it willpower.

Many a man thinks he's going places when he's really being taken.

The average man's idea of a good sermon is one that goes over his head and hits a neighbor.

Conscience is that still, small voice that tells you what other people should do.

People go on vacation to forget things—and when they get there they find out they did.

The disappearance of the hatpin is the only successful case of disarmament in history.

The way things are being speeded up, it won't be long before a person can take a two-week vacation in four days.

Solitude is often the reward of punctuality.

A budget helps you pay as you go—if you don't go anywhere.

If you want the world to beat a path to your door, just lie down to take a nap.

Well-bred folks are seldom crusty.

Never make the same mistake twice—make a new one.

A genius is a crackpot until he hits the jackpot.

It must be wonderful to be young enough to know everything.

Forty years ago when a fellow said something about retiring he was talking about going to bed.

A miser is a home-loving body who rarely goes buy-buy.

Kindness always pays, but it usually pays best when it is not done for pay.

No one is ever too old to learn, but many put it off.

Usually the absent member of the bridge club is the one who gets the most slams.

Many a man's idea of charity is to give unto others the advice he won't use himself.

A man may be a 20-ton truck in the office and only a 2-wheel trailer at home.

A friend is a person who tells you all the nice things you always knew about yourself.

Why complain about getting old? When we stop growing older, we're dead.

A toastmaster at a dinner is the person who gets up to tell you the best part of the evening is over.

No one is too busy to talk about how busy he is.

Life may begin at forty, but so does rheumatism.

We need not all think alike, but we should all think.

If you know what time a young man turns in, you can often tell how he will turn out.

The world measures success by your ability to get along with some people and ahead of others.

In the old days before inflation, you could be down to your last dollar and have enough to pay for at least three meals.

Many of us are like the letter "B"—in debt, with no need for it.

There isn't much to talk about at most parties until a few people have left.

Sometimes the fellow who says he is busy is just confused.

Say, that Zip Code is really working. Now, any letter posted before noon is delivered the following morning—give or take a few weeks.

Sign in a loan company office: "Ask us about our plans for owning your home."

Some practical person should write a book on "How to Get Out of Doing It Yourself."

He proposed on his knees with a speech tender-sweet, and it took him ten years to get back on his feet!

A major airline announces a new economy class. It will show home movies.

Appearances are deceiving—a dollar looks the same as it did ten years ago.

If machines get too powerful, we can organize them into committees, and that will do them in.

If you think twice before you speak, you'll never get into the conversation.

Even if money grew on trees, a few smart folks would still get most of it.

Of course college students get out of line now and then—you can't picket all the time.

What happens if you mix a bottle of ink eradicator with a bottle of ink?

Some after-dinner speakers are so windy they should be called gusts of honor.

An honest golfer is one who tells the "hole" truth.

If you want children to listen, talk softly to somebody else.

Parents never appreciate parents until they are.

CHAPTER 2

IDEAS FOR SPEECHES AND SERMONS

Traffic Jams

We fuss and we fume with the traffic of too many cars on the street, but the snarls of the carts in today's supermarts have all other traffic jams beat.

Salute!

A toast to the steadfast, reliable man, the man who's square and true; he won't promise to do more than he can, but he does what he says he'll do. He's not very clever and often quite blunt, without either polish or air; he never tries to "put up a front," but when you need him, he's there.

So here's to the man on whom you rely, and here's to his lasting success! "May his species continue to multiply, and his shadow never grow less."

Autumn

The feeling of fall comes to me very suddenly sometimes. There comes a day when cold grayish clouds cover the sky, the trees are shaken by cold, raw wind, and rarer birds are gone, and the more hardy are flocking, and as you walk or ride along, there suddenly comes to you a vision of a fire in a grate, of nuts and books and papers, and the charm of indoors beside one's own hearth. The summer is gone and the sterner season makes itself felt.—*John Burroughs*

Attitude

It's not the body's posture, but the heart's attitude that counts, when we pray.—*Billy Graham*

Three Inscriptions

Above the triple doorways of the Cathedral of Milan there are three inscriptions. Over one is carved a beautiful wreath of roses and underneath is the legend, "All that which pleases is but for a moment." Over the other door is sculptured a cross with the words, "All that which troubles is but for a moment." Over the great central entrance is the inscription, "That only is important which is eternal."

If

If every little grain of sand were like a cannonball—how should we ever navigate, go anywhere at all? And if the tiny drops of rain that water thirsty ground where foaming, splashing bucketfuls, should not we all be drowned? Then, too, the blades of velvet grass that make our lovely lawn—what should we do if they were large, just like our blades of corn?

So, if you're small and unrenowned, don't take the time to grumble. Just thank your fate that you won't cause someone to drown or stumble!—*Sunshine Magazine*

The World Will Survive

James Russell Lowell once wrote: "Let us be of good cheer, remembering that the misfortunes hardest to bear are those which never come. The world has outlived much, and will outlive a great deal more, and men have contrived to be happy in it. It has shown the strength of its constitution in nothing more than in surviving the quack medicines it has tried."

The Lady With the Lamp

The "Lady With the Lamp," probably America's number one tourist attraction, has stood on Liberty Island, formerly

Bedloe Island, in New York Harbor since 1886, when formal dedication services were held on October 28, with President Cleveland and the sculptor Frederic Auguste Bartholdi present. The Statue of Liberty was a gift from the French people to the United States, commemorating the alliance of the two nations during the American Revolution, and attests their everlasting international friendship. These were President Cleveland's dedicatory words: "We will not forget that Liberty has here made her home; or shall her chosen altar be neglected." And thus it became a shrine to freedom.

Price Controls

After failure of attempts to regulate prices during the American Revolution, the Continental Congress decided in 1788 that price control laws did more harm than good: "It hath been found by experience," said a resolution adopted by the Congress, "That limitation in the price of commodities is not only ineffective for the purpose proposed, but likewise productive of very evil consequences, to the great detriment of the public service, and to the very grievous oppression of the individuals."

Vision

An old man going a long highway
Came at the evening cold and gray,
To a chasm vast and deep and wide.
The old man crossed in the twilight dim,
The sullen stream had no fears for him;
But he turned when safe on the other side,
And built a bridge to span the tide.

"Old man," said a fellow pilgrim near,
"You are wasting your time with building here.
You never again will pass this way,

Your journey will end with the closing day.
You have crossed the chasm deep and wide,
Why build you this bridge at the evening tide?"

The builder lifted his old gray head.
"Good friend, in the way that I've come," he said,
"There followeth after me today
A youth whose feet must pass this way.
This stream that has been as naught to me
To the fair-haired youth might a pitfall be.
He, too, must cross in the twilight dim.
Good friend, I am building this bridge for him."

—*Author Unknown in Worden & Risberg bulletin*

A Tribute At Death
Readings From the Scriptures

Our help is in the name of the Lord, who made heaven and earth.

The eternal God is thy Refuge, and underneath are the everlasting arms.

Psalm 121:

I will lift up mine eyes unto the hills,
From whence cometh my help.
My help cometh from the Lord,
Which made heaven and earth.

The Lord is thy keeper:
The Lord is thy shade upon thy right hand.

The Lord shall preserve thee from all evil:
He shall preserve thy soul.
The Lord shall preserve thy going out and thy coming in
From this time forth, and even for evermore.

Psalm 23:

The Lord is my Shepherd; I shall not want.
He maketh me to lie down in green pastures;
He leadeth me beside the still waters.
He restoreth my soul:
He leadeth me in the paths of righteousness for His
name's sake.

St. John 14:

Jesus said: Let not your heart be troubled; ye believe in God, believe also in Me. In My Father's house are many mansions: if it were not so, I would have told you. I go to prepare a place for you . . .

I am the way, the truth, and the life; no man cometh unto the Father, but by Me . . .

Peace I leave with you, My peace I give unto you: not as the world giveth, give I unto you. Let not your heart be troubled, neither let it be afraid.

Deuteronomy 31:

Be strong and of good courage, fear not! Jehovah, thy God, He it is that doth go with thee. He will not fail thee, nor forsake thee.—*The Reverend James W. Harris, Northminster, Presbyterian Church, Evanston, Illinois*

Adolescence

A high school girl has the energy of a miniature atomic bomb, the lungs of an auctioneer, the curiosity of a cat, the imagination of Edgar A. Poe, the fault-finding ability of a bookkeeper, the irresponsibility of a butterfly, and the friendliness of a bus driver.—*Joyce Bass, Chatterbox, Geo. Washington High School, Danville, Virginia*

America's Strength

It is a prayer that has been on every heart. And while the statesmen of the world are seeking paths to peace, it should be in the heart of every loyal American just as earnestly as it was in the days of peace. What is the strength of America? What are the secrets of our nation's power? Wherein lie the resources which guarantee the perpetuity of the American way of life?

The agriculturalist might have you believe America's strength lies in its soil.

The merchant would say that a nation's power rests in its commerce.

The manufacturer might assert that it is in technology, in machinery, and in the skilled labor to operate plants to produce manufactured products.

The politician might contend that a nation's strength is in statecraft, in astuteness and acumen in national policies.

The educator might declare that knowledge is power, and that our country's greatness is in its learning, its science, the products of the laboratory.

The militarist most likely would insist that a nation is great according to its weapons.

But America's real strength is in the character of her people, in the moral and spiritual fiber or ties which root in the home.

The hand that rocks the cradle is still greater than the one that wields the scepter. A nation's strength depends upon the quality of its home life.—*Youth Progress*

Bible

Voltaire said that in 100 years the Bible would be a forgotten book found only in museums. When the 100 years were up, Voltaire's home was occupied by the Geneva Bible Society. —*Friendly Thoughts*

Reform

A reformer is one who sets forth cheerfully toward sure defeat.—*Richard S. Childs*

Making a Decision

If you wait too long to make a decision, you are not making a decision at all. You are avoiding one.

Our National Life

We want serenity of faith without agony, victory without struggle, solvency without taxes, leadership without criticism, peace without sacrifice, and salvation without conviction. —*James Reston*

A Prayer for My Pastor

Let me be a pillar of strength to help hold him up and not a thorn in his flesh to sap his strength, nor a burden on his back to pull him down.

Let me lift his hands without placing shackles around them.

Let me give him my help, that he may devote more time to working for the salvation of others, and less time in gratifying my vanity. Let me work for him as the pastor of all the members.

Let me be unselfish in what I do for him and not selfish in demanding that he do more for me.

Let me strive to serve him and the church more and be happy as he serves me less and the church and others more. Amen.—*Anonymous*

A Philosophy of Life

To be called upon to set forth my philosophy of life in a brief statement is indeed a challenging and sobering assignment—an opportunity, however, to attempt to summarize in a few sentences the essence of what I believe to be a good and useful life.

As all of us must realize, if we pause for a moment in our crowded and sometimes frantic day-to-day schedules, we are living in a dangerously materialistic age. Too often ethics and principles are disregarded or compromised in our hectic struggle for more and more wealth, prestige and power. Too seldom do we stop to consider where we are going, what we believe to be really important, and how we can improve ourselves as human beings so that we will be better able to help others.

What is it that sets apart men like Abraham Lincoln, Mahatma Gandhi and Albert Schweitzer? Unusual ability, of course; but many individuals of extraordinary ability have fallen far short of these great men. To me it seems that these men, and all men and women who are truly outstanding, have a combination of five basic characteristics:

1. A deep-rooted faith that will sustain them through the trials and crises of their lives.

2. A genuine humility, coupled with a sincere respect for their fellow men.

3. An instinctive sense of fairness and integrity.

4. A determination to develop as fully as humanly possible whatever talents God has given them.

5. And finally, a willingness to struggle and sacrifice for what they unselfishly believe to be right—the antithesis of apathy and smug complacency.

In my opinion this final factor—the willingness to stand up and fight for what we believe in, regardless of selfish or materialistic consequences—is where we most often fail, for unfortunately apathy tends to flourish during periods of prosperity.

By pointing out what I most admire in others I have tried to set forth the basic ingredients of my own philosophy. It is unlikely that a person whose life is based upon a "philosophy" of this kind will find luxury and ease, but I am confident he will have great inner satisfaction and peace of mind, as well as a good and useful life.—*Christopher M. Wilson, Executive Vice President and Cashier, The First National Bank of Chicago*

The Gift of the Pilgrims

The Pilgrim Fathers came to America seeking religious freedom. But the idea that they were sober-faced, graybearded religious fanatics is completely erroneous. They were, for the most part, vigorous young men and women in their twenties and thirties, whose devotion to religion did not make them sad or solemn. They appreciated the good things of life. They loved to sing and play at sports and games of skill.

The Pilgrims liked color in their clothes. A study of their wills has revealed the ownership of such finery as a "satin" suit, "sky colored garters," a "cap with silver lace." There were numerous blue, red, and green cloaks and smocks. William Brewster wore a violet suit for important occasions.

But they never let these pleasures blind them to the spiritual values they needed to survive. When they were preparing to sail to the New World, pessimistic friends drew up a terrifying list of things that could go wrong—the ship might sink, disease might wipe them out, savage Indians might do likewise, adding hideous tortures to their fate. The Pilgrims listened to it all and admitted that any one of these things was possible. But that was no reason for refusing to set sail. With the help of God, all the terrors and dangers of the future could be met and overcome by "answerable courages."

As long as America retains this most precious of Pilgrim gifts, we will continue to have cause to give thanks.—*Sunshine Magazine*

Wonder

Socrates, when the young Theatetus was introduced to him as a lad of brilliant promise, said to him that he felt sure he had thought a great deal. The boy answered, "Oh, no—not that, but at least I have wondered a great deal." "Ah, that shows the lover of wisdom," Socrates said, "for wisdom begins in wonder."—*Plato*

God

God does not die on the day when we cease to believe in a personal diety, but we die on the day when our lives cease to be illumined by the steady radiance, renewed daily, of a wonder, the source of which is beyond all reason.—*Dag Hammarskjold*

God

If we could solve all the mysteries of the Universe, we would be co-equal with God. Every drop of ocean shares its glory but is not the ocean.—*Mahatma Gandhi*

Man

Yet Thou hast made him but little lower than the angels,
And hast crowned him with glory and honor.
Thou hast made him to have dominion over the works of Thy
    Hands;
Thou hast put all things under his feet.—Psalms 8:6-7

Lonely

"Are you not lonely out here?" asked a visitor of a lighthouse keeper on an isolated reef. "Not since I saved my first man," came the swift answer.—*Harry Emerson Fosdick*

War and Peace

If we could internationally display on this front some of the imagination and initiative, determination and sacrifice, that we show in respect of defense planning and development the outlook would be more hopeful than it is. The grim fact, however, is that we prepare for war like precocious giants and for peace like retarded pygmies.—*Lester B. Pearson*

Human Individual

We must broaden the frontiers of our loyalties, never forgetting as we do so that it is the human individual, and not the state or any other community, in whom ultimate sovereignty is vested.—*J. William Fulbright*

Noblest Question

The noblest question in the world is, "What good may I do in it?"—*Benjamin Franklin*

There Is No Other Thing

Do not weep, my children. I am not going very far, and I shall see you from there; you will only have to look up at night and you will see me smile . . . Thus God apportions things . . . He sees us all, and He knows what He does amid His great stars . . . Love each other well and always. There is no other thing in the world but that; love one another . . . My children, I can no longer see clearly. I had other things to say to you, but no matter. Think of me sometimes . . . I don't know what ails me! I see light. Come nearer yet. I die happy. Let me lay my hands on your beloved heads.—*Victor Hugo*

Loneliness

Pray that your loneliness may spur you into finding something to live for, great enough to die for.—*Dag Hammarskjold*

Inner Values

What the businessman needs most today, it seems to me, is a sense of inner values. He needs to know the purposes of his life. He needs to know the objectives toward which his life is moving. He needs to have his own sense of values by which he can determine his own achievements—because, unless you know what you are trying to do, you can't keep score. At the end you don't know how you have done.—*Clarence B. Randall*

Marriage

The best marriages, like the best lives, were both happy and unhappy. There is even a kind of necessary tension, a certain tautness between the partners that gave the marriage strength, like the tautness of a full sail. You went forward on it.—*Anne Morrow Lindbergh*

Bored

The mistake a lot of guys make, they're always pushin' their kids. "Don't just sit there," they tell 'em. "Go do something. Go play ball, go watch TV, go annoy the neighbors." Not me. I see to it my kids have a chance to get bored.—*Robert Wells*

The Home

Moral and religious education consist in training the feelings and daily habits . . . It is the home, the family, which gives us the moral or religious education we really receive . . . —*John Stuart Mill*

Kindness

Abraham Lincoln was questioned by one of his advisors as follows: "Mr. President, I cannot understand you. You treat your enemies with such kindness. It would seem to me that you should want to destroy them."

"My dear fellow," said the President, "I do destroy my enemy when I make him into a friend."—*Anonymous*

The Major Problem

The major problem on earth is not the bomb. The bomb is actually the product of the problem. The main problem is that the human imagination has not yet expanded to the point where it comprehends its own essential utility. People are not yet aware of themselves as a single interdependent species requiring the proper performance of certain vital services if the human race is to be sustained. They have developed a world reach without a world consciousness.—*Norman Cousins*

What Man Owes to God

In a century in which so many of the mentors of the public mind—from the psychiatrists to the ad-men—speak to us in terms of "what we owe to ourselves," may there not indeed have been a slackening of devotion compared with those days, not so long distant, when what man owes to God and his neighbor was a common theme of public discourse?—*Adlai E. Stevenson*

Freedom

Freedom is an individual word. If we want to enjoy it, and fight for it, we must be prepared to extend it to everyone. —*Wendell L. Willkie*

Self-Examination

The first question written on the blackboard was, "Which of the required readings in this course did you find least interesting?" Then, after members of the class had had minutes in which to expatiate on what was certainly to many a congenial topic, he wrote the second question: "To what defect in yourself do you attribute this lack of interest?"—*Joseph Wood Krutch*

Smart or Wise

The difference between a smart man and a wise one is this: A smart man can work his way out of a difficulty that a wise man will not get into in the first place.—*Saul Lieberman*

Advantages

"Whenever you feel like criticizing anyone . . . just remember that all the people in this world haven't had the advantages that you've had.—*F. Scott Fitzgerald*

God

I will tell you, scholar, I have heard a grave divine say that God has two dwellings, one in heaven and the other in a meek and thankful heart.—*Izaak Walton*

Vision

. . . I want somebody on that hilltop or its equivalent who can be thinking and looking far ahead and who can prod me into doing the things that it would be easier not to do. Don't try to think of things that are politically shrewd . . . Try to think of the next generation.—*Adlai E. Stevenson*

Courage

When the morning's freshness has been replaced by the weariness of midday, when the leg muscles quiver under the strain, the climb seems endless, and, suddenly, nothing will go quite as you wish—it is then that you must not hesitate.
—*Dag Hammarskjold*

Forgiveness

I must forgive the lovelessness, the hatred, the slander, the fraud, the arrogance which I encounter, since I myself have so often lacked love, hated, slandered, defrauded, and been arrogant. I must forgive without noise or fuss. In general I do not even get as far as being merely just.—*Albert Schweitzer*

Wonderful Creation

There are times when I feel like a boy. As long as you are able to admire and to love, you are young. And there is so much to admire and to love . . Look at the sea, the sky, trees, flowers! A single tree—what a miracle it is! What a fantastic, wonderful creation this world is, with such diversity! That is the law of nature—diversity.—*Pablo Casals*

New Horizons

"The greatest honor history can bestow is the title of peacemaker. This honor now beckons America—the chance to help lead the world at last out of the valley of turmoil and onto that high ground of peace that man has dreamed of since the dawn of civilization . . .

"We seek an open world—open to ideas, open to the exchange of goods and people—a world in which no people, great or small, will live in angry isolation . . .

"As we explore the reaches of space, let us go to the new worlds together—not as new worlds to be conquered, but as a new adventure to be shared.

"With those who are willing to join, let us cooperate to reduce the burden of arms, to strengthen the structure of peace, to lift up the poor and the hungry . . ."—*President Richard M. Nixon, Inaugural Address, January 20, 1969*

Capitalist

Johnny and Tim used to be laborers.

Both cut lawns. Both used customers' hand mowers. Each could do one big lawn a day, and got $2 for it.

Tim spent his $2 on movies and candy. Johnny saved some money, borrowed some more, and bought a power mower. Now he can cut five lawns a day, and so makes $10. He puts aside $2 a day to pay back his loan, and $1 toward another mower when this one wears out.

He still has seven dollars where he used to have two, and is helping more people get their lawns cut when they want them. Yet some enemies of business would say that that shows Johnny is too big; he should be limited in the number of people he can serve.

These same strange enemies would prevent Johnny from setting aside $1 a day out of his own earnings, to buy a new mower when this one wears out. (Of course, that means Johnny would go back to hand labor at $2 a day, and fewer people would be served—but these strange people don't care about that.)

And some people say Johnny should be forced to share his $7 with Tim so Tim can keep on spending his $2 for movies and candy for himself.—*Evans Echoes*

Appreciation

That efficiency as well as a pleasant working atmosphere is the result of appreciation or praise has been given some weight in recent university tests.

One example: Students were split into three groups for a test project. The first group was encouraged and praised; the second was ignored; the third treated in a shabby manner—given a diet of nothing but criticism. The ignored group accomplished the least, the criticized group made a little headway, but the praised group achieved outstanding progress.

The lesson has been stated before—perhaps eons ago: If appreciation indicates a man is better than he is, he may often be inspired to do better than he thought he could. An old but true motto for management—in business or out of it.—*Evans Echoes*

An Irish Toast

"May the blessing of light be on you, light without and light within. May the blessed sunshine shine on you, and warm your heart till it glows like a great peat fire, so that the stranger may come and warm himself by it, and become a friend.

"And may the light shine out of the two eyes of you, like candles set in two windows of a house, bidding the wanderer to come out of the storm.

"And may the blessing of the rain be on you, the soft sweet rain. May it fall upon your spirit so that all your little flowers may spring up and shed their sweetness on the air.

"And may the blessing of the great rains be on you. May they beat upon your spirit and wash it fair and clean, and leave many a shining pool where the blue of heaven shines, and sometimes a star.

"And may the blessing of the earth be on you, the great round earth. May you have a kindly greeting for those you pass as you're going along the roads.

"May the earth be soft under you when you rest upon it, tired at the end of a day; and may it rest easy over you when, at the last, you lie out under it. May it rest so lightly over you that your soul may be off from under it quickly, and up, and off, and on its way to God.

"And now may the Lord bless you. And bless you kindly."

Changing Character of the Nation

Looking back for a moment at the time of the American Revolution—less than five percent of our population lived in cities—and in only two cities—New York and Philadelphia—were there as many as 30,000 inhabitants. As late as 1910—eighty percent of our population still lived on farms. In short—for most of history—the few cities we had were only small islands in a sea of rural life. Today, however—the United States is seventy percent urban—and there are nineteen metropolitan regions in the country with a population of a million or more. Technology has given us a highly mobile population moving to a new place of residence every year. Those who choose the profession of elected public office must cope with the fact that there will be nearly a forty percent change in their constituents when they run for reelection every two years. So not only are we members of a highly mobile population—but one wherein the preferences for urban life have given rise to the fact that seventy percent of our population now lives on one percent of the land.—*Dr. Lucius P. Gregg, Jr.*

Amazing Cities

While New York has the largest population, Los Angeles is the most spread out with a land area of over 450 square miles.

The highest state capital is Denver, Colorado, "The Mile High City," where the altitude on the steps of the capitol building is exactly 5,280 feet! Our newest state capital is Honolulu, Hawaii, which also has more city-owned parks than any other—3,000 of them! Juneau, Alaska, has the distinction of being the northernmost capital and the coldest city in the United States, with average temperature of 40.1°F.

While some cities are famous for their size, others are equally famous for other superlatives. The highest capital in the world, before the conquest by China, was Lhasa in Tibet with an elevation of 12,087 feet above sea level. Jericho, now called Ariha, in Jordan, is the oldest known walled town: it may have been inhabited as early as 7800 B.C. The world's oldest city, Damascus, Syria, has been continuously inhabited since 2000 B.C.

Many cities around the world attract visitors to see their architectural marvels of bygone days. Such structures as the Taj Mahal, Chartres Cathedral, and the Egyptian pyramids have withstood the test of time and continue to inspire modern architects.

Many other cities have become well-known by their nicknames, such as Paris, "The City of Light." Montreal, the capital of the Canadian province of Quebec, is often called "The City of Saints," because so many of the streets there are named after saints. Strausbourg, in northern France, is sometimes referred to as "The City of Bells." "The City of the Three Kings" is Cologne, Germany, which is reputed to the burial place of the Magi.

Rome is known as "The City of the Seven Hills," and "The Eternal City." It was said that Agrippa, during the reign of Augustus, converted it "from a city of brick huts to one of marble palaces."—*Evans Echoes*

Teach These Words

On the occasion of the birth of her first granddaughter, a very wise old mother wrote the mother of the child as follows:

"Teach her as many of the 700,000 words of the English language as you can, but be sure she knows the greatest word is God; the longest word, eternity; the swiftest word, time; the nearest word, now; the darkest word, sin; the meanest word, hypocrisy; and the deepest word, soul."

Never Finished

When I lived in Washington—every day I would ride past the Washington Monument and the Lincoln Memorial—and I would often think of the men and the events they commemorate. But as I look at the perfection of the monuments—I try to remember—and I ask you to remember—that this nation was conceived and designed by human beings—imperfect as you and I are imperfect—capable of mistakes, even as you and I—subject to weariness and doubt and confusion, as all of us are. But with all their human fallibility—they had the courage in their heart to believe that man might one day create a free and just society. And that made the difference.

Our efforts must have the vision and the steadiness of purpose to try and make an imperfect world better. That is hard work—and it is never finished.

A nation is never finished. You can't build it and then leave it standing as the Pharaohs did at the pyramids. It has to be built and rebuilt. It has to be recreated in each generation by believing and concerned men and women.—*Dr. Lucius P. Gregg, Jr.*

Labor, Capital or Brains

Andrew Carnegie was once asked by a reporter what he considered most important in industry: labor, capital, or brains? With a laugh Carnegie replied: "Which is the most important leg of a three-legged stool?"

Panic Stop

You've heard it!

There's an agonizing screech as a foot slams hard on the

brake pedal. Then a second or two of suspense, which may or may not be followed by a horrendous crash and the clattering of broken glass on the pavement.

You've seen it!

There are those long black marks where tortured tires left their marks on the road.

That's a panic stop!

Don't let anybody tell you that panic stops happen because an emergency situation pops up suddenly and unexpectedly and there's nothing to do but hit the brakes hard.

When you hear this you can figure one of two things happened. Either the driver was riding the tail of the vehicle in front of him and not paying much attention to that vehicle or the one in front of it, or he delayed braking although he may have seen a potentially hazardous situation ahead (car on side road, children playing near the street, etc.).

Those are two things of which smart drivers aren't guilty. —*National Safety Council*

A House or a Home

There is all the difference in the world between a "house" and a "home." A house is something material whether it be a palace or a cottage, a split-level or a shack. A home is something more. It is the total contribution of love on the part of each one dwelling within it. It is a sanctuary wherein the real presence of family life and family love dwells.—*Evans Echoes*

Self-Respect

Self-respect cannot be hunted. It cannot be purchased. It is never for sale. It comes to us when we are alone, in quiet moments, in quiet places, when we suddenly realize that, knowing the good, we have done it; knowing the beautiful, we have served it; knowing the truth, we have spoken it.—*Whitney Griswold*

Freedom

Let us live our lives so that we may proclaim to the whole world: Individual freedom is our creed—national freedom is our heritage—world freedom is our goal.—*J. Edgar Hoover, United Evangelical Action*

Education

Today's youngsters, as every parent knows, can recite TV commercials long before they learn to read. Francis Keppel, former U.S. Commissioner of Education, opined recently that teachers in the primary grades ought to keep this in mind. "I wonder," he observed, "if the look-see teachers ever thought that the first word a child would learn to spell would be Schlitz."—*John Scanlon, Saturday Review*

Loss of Time

"And what is most neglected and most regretted?" asked the Magi.

"Time," answered Zadig. "All men neglect it, and all men regret the loss of it, and nothing can be done without it."

You Better Think Twice

If someone should offer to give you a billion dollars in one dollar bills, if you promise to count it, would you accept it? Well, it would take you about sixty years, eight hours per day, three hundred and sixty-five days in the year, to do the job. And chances are, before you were half through, you would be broken in health.

A Pleasing Welcome

An unexpected but pleasing welcome greets guests in their rooms in the Riceland Hotel in Stuttgart, Arkansas. The hospitality expressed encourages them to return. Here are the words of good wishes.

"Greetings, Traveler! In ancient times, there was a prayer for the 'stranger within our gates.' We hope that God will grant you peace and rest while you are under our roof. May this room be your 'second' home. May those you love be near you in thoughts and dreams. Even though we may not get to know you, we hope that you will be as comfortable and happy as if you were in your own house. May the business that brought you our way prosper. May every call you make and every message you receive add to your joy. When you leave, may your journey be safe. We are all travelers 'from birth to death.' We travel between the eternities. May these days be pleasant for you; profitable for society, helpful for those you meet, and a joy to those who know and love you the very best."

Brevity

George Washington's second inaugural address was the shortest inaugural speech given by any President of the United States—just 134 words.

The Federal Debt?

And what comes after millions, billions, and trillions? It is quadrillions, quintillions, sextillions, septillions, octillions, nonillions, decillions, undecillions, duodecillions, tredecillions, quattuordecillions, quindecillions, sexdecillions, septendecillions, octodecillions, novemdecillions, vigintillions, and centillions.

Injustice

Search all your parks in all your cities. You'll find no statues to committees.

Mass Production

Mass production, the backbone of our economy and our standard of living, is not new in America. In 1798, when each army rifle had to be made by hand—each part to fit one gun and one gun only—Eli Whitney evolved an unheard of method of speedily forging and stamping out "standard" interchangeable parts and assembling them later.

Using the Whitney "mass production" method in 1807, a New England clockmaker began manufacturing 5,000 clocks a year instead of four, and selling them for $5 instead of $25. The idea has been going strong ever since.

God and Man

An old Vermont farmer was walking home from the village when he met a stranger. The farmer noted that his companion had a stern face and talked with sanctimonious language.

At one point the stranger stopped and pointed a long, lean finger at the farmer and asked, "Have you made your peace with God?"

The old Vermonter looked for a moment at his companion. Then he said abruptly, "We ain't come to no open break yet."
—*The Reverend Paul M. Humphreys, Church Management*

Keep Facing It!

A tramp, when asked about his philosophy of life, replied, "I turn my back to the wind." That probably is why he was a tramp. Following the line of least resistance is what makes rivers and many men crooked. A man cannot drift to success.

In contrast to this philosophy is the statement which Captain MacWhite spoke to his mate in Joseph Conrad's immortal tale of the sea, "Typhoon." In the midst of a great storm, MacWhite said: "Keep facing it! They may say what they like —the heaviest seas run with the wind. Always facing it! That's the way to get through it!"—*Sunshine Magazine*

Religion

A famous story of French history recounts that Voltaire, a notorious infidel, was standing beside a friend one day on the streets of Paris where there passed by a religious procession carrying a crucifix. Voltaire lifted his hat. His friend noticing this unexpected gesture said: "What is this? Are you reconciled to God?" "No," said Voltaire with sharp irony. "We salute, but we do not speak."—*The Reverend Richard R. Potter, "Are We Off Speaking Terms With God?" Christian Observer*

Back to the First Grade Salt Mine

Two first graders were standing outside the school one morning. "Do you think," asked one, "that thermonuclear projectiles will always be affected by radiation belts?"

"No," said the other. "Once a force enters space . . ."

The school bell rang. "Well," said the first youngster, "here we go, back to the old bead stringing."

Five Indispensables

"If I had a son," once wrote J. Edgar Hoover, "I believe I could help him most by providing him with these five indispensables: a personal example to follow, an understanding of the importance of restraint and ideals, a sense of discipline, a pride in his heritage, and a challenge to meet."

What Worries Him

It isn't the things in the Bible I don't understand that worry me; it's the things I do understand.—*Mark Twain*

Worth Thinking About

Courage is not the absence of fear—it is the mastery of it.—*Confucius*

Serving Others

You must give some time to your fellow men. Even if it's a little thing, do something for others—something for which you get no pay but the privilege of doing it.—*Albert Schweitzer*

Poverty and Productivity

I'm all in favor of the idealism of youth, but I have been getting the impression that youth is necessarily characterized by intelligence, compassion and the other virtues, and that age seems to impart little but insensitivity, ignorance and pragmatism. This concerns me. Our perspective may be getting out of balance. An ideal is something for which we strive, but the accomplishment requires skill, perseverance and patience.

Poverty cannot be overcome by compassion. Compassion is a worthy and necessary virtue, but by itself it neither nourishes the body nor protects it from the elements. The continued good health of industry, and increased productivity, are our best hope of ministering to the needs of those who are the object of compassion.—*E. Victor Milione*

Doing Business

Unless a company can return a profit and reinvest for modern equipment and the like, it won't be around very long to "do good." But this does not mean that we cannot be compassionate at the same time. The very process of "doing business" should be directed toward the most basic and sometimes urgent needs of human beings.—*Gene E. Bradley*

Infinite

The sun is so large that if it were hollow, it could contain more than one million worlds the size of our earth. There are stars in space so large that they could easily hold five hundred million suns the size of ours. There are about 100 billion stars in the average galaxy, and there are at least 100 million galaxies in known space.

Ten Commandments for the Battle of Life

B. C. Forbes, the founder and longtime editor of *Forbes Magazine,* drew up the following ten commandments for those earnestly seeking to fight successfully the battle of life:

First—Study.
Second—Sweat.

Third—Keep accounts.
Fourth—Save systematically.
Fifth—Take out life insurance.
Sixth—Buy your own home.
Seventh—Investment in sound securities.
Eighth—Educate your children.
Ninth—Travel.
Tenth—Give generously.

Asking for Help

The story is told of a small boy trying very hard to lift a heavy stone. His father happened by and noted the son's failure, and said to him, "Are you using all your strength?"

"Yes, I am," the boy exclaimed impatiently.

"No," the father replied, "you are not. You haven't asked me to help."

Two Rules of Life

There are two great rules of life. The one is general and the other particular. The first is that everyone can, in the end, get what he wants if he only tries. That is a general rule. The particular rule is that every individual, more or less, is an exception to the general rule.—*Samuel Butler*

Actions Speak Louder

Dr. Francis Bower, New York school psychologist, commenting on actions and attitudes of adults that he says tend to confuse and disillusion young people, pointed out these facts: "We talk about building close family relationships, and send the children to nursery schools at three and to summer schools, recreational programs, and summer camps for the remainder of their childhood years.

"We tell him (the adolescent) to respect authority while we disparage our public officials. We tell him to obey the law while we attempt to bribe a policeman or fix a traffic ticket.

We tell him to be decent and honest and, above all, upright—while we cheat on our income tax.

"We stress the importance of scientific and academic achievement and then make millionaires of our entertainers and paupers of our professors."

Leisure

It is the evenings, the holidays, the leisure hours in life that truly make for character and success. The great strain doesn't come during the busy day. If you want to find the worth of a man, find out how he spends his leisure moments.

The Moments to Come

They do me wrong who say I come no more
When once I knock and fail to find you in;
For every day I stand outside your door,
And bid you wake, and rise to fight and win.

Wail not for precious chances passed away,
Weep not for golden ages on the wane;
Each night I burn the records of the day;
At sunrise every soul is born again.

Laugh like a boy at splendors that have sped,
To vanished joys be blind and deaf and dumb;
My judgments seal the dead past with its dead;
But never bind a moment yet to come.

Though deep in mire wring not your hands and weep;
I lend my arm to all who say "I can!"
No shamefaced outcast ever sank so deep
But yet might rise and be again a man!

Dost thou behold thy lost youth all aghast?
Dost reel from righteous retribution's blow?
Then turn from blotted archives of the past
And find the future's pages white as snow.

Art thou a mourner? Rouse thee from thy spell!
Art thou a sinner? Sins may be forgiven;
Each morning gives the wings to flee from hell,
Each night a star to guide thy feet to heaven!
—Walter Malone (1866-1915)
From a bulletin of Worden & Risberg

Prayer

It is better in prayer to have a heart without words than words without a heart.—*Mahatma Gandhi*

Sense of Proportion

One of the most valuable gifts for a man, or nation, to possess is a sense of proportion—the common sense, that is, to know the order of priority in which to put or take the manifold concerns of life. —*Arthur Bryant, Illustrated London News*

Solitude

I love to be alone. I never found the companion that was so companionable as solitude.—*Henry David Thoreau*

Freedom

The freedom that counts is simply what is in the minds and hearts of millions of free people. It is nothing more than the total of the feelings of people as they are expressed in the way we, the people, deal with our own families and our own neighbors and associates.—*Adlai E. Stevenson*

Well Governed

What is a city but a collection of houses? How then can a city be well governed, when there is no government in the separate houses, and neither child nor servant is obedient? Likewise, what is a province but a collection of cities, towns and villages? When, therefore, the families are badly controlled, how can the province be well governed? . . . Where father and mother rule badly and let the children have their own way, there neither city, town, village, district, principality, kingdom nor empire can be well and peacefully governed.—*Martin Luther*

Ten Traffic Rules for Children

Here are ten rules for children to observe as their part in "playing safe."

1. Start to school early so you won't have to rush.
2. Plan the safest trip to and from school, and follow it every day.
3. Cross at the crossings, never in the middle of the block.
4. Cross only with the safe lights.
5. Be alert at all times when crossing streets.
6. Obey the officer or safety-patrol boy at the crossing.
7. Don't hitch rides or dart out onto the street from behind parked cars or hedges.
8. Play in safe places—playgrounds, play streets, vacant lots —not on dangerous streets.
9. Ride bicycles on the right side of roadways, and obey traffic signals and stop signs.
10. On highways always walk on the left, facing traffic.

Masterpieces

The three greatest masterpieces in literature, it is sometimes said, are the Lord's Prayer, the Twenty-Third Psalm, and Lincoln's Gettsyburg Address. Incidentally, recall their wording:

"Our Father which art in Heaven, hallowed be thy name."

"The Lord is my shepherd; I shall not want."

"Fourscore and seven years ago."

Not a three-syllable word in them; hardly any two-syllable words. All the greatest things in human life are one-syllable things—love, joy, hope, home, child, wife, trust, faith, God. All great things are simple.

Life

You can make more friends in two months by becoming interested in other people than you can in two years by trying to get other people interested in you.—*Dale Carnegie*

Fact

Every man has a right to his opinion, but no man has a right to be wrong in his facts.—*Bernard Baruch*

Man's mind stretched to a new idea never goes back to its original dimensions.—*Oliver Wendell Holmes*

An Hour a Day

If you devote but one hour a day to an engrossing project, you will give it 365 hours a year, or the equivalent of more than 45 full working days of eight hours each. This is like adding one and a half months of productive living to every year of life! Yet when we talk about an hour a day of privacy for self-development, the reply is apt to be: "I'm too busy. I work all day. When I come home I'm exhausted."

Admittedly it is not easy. It requires resolution. The trick is to create the hour, then use it wisely.—*Sunshine Magazine*

Correct Analysis

A disgruntled schoolteacher handed in her resignation with the following comment: "In our public schools the teachers are afraid of the principal, the principals are afraid of the superintendents, the superintendents are afraid of the board, the board members are afraid of the parents, the parents are afraid of the children, and the children are afraid of nobody."

Time

"What of all things in the world is the longest and the shortest?" Zadig was asked by the Magi.

"Time," answered Zadig, "for nothing is longer, since time is a measure of eternity; and nothing is shorter, since our time is insufficient for the accomplishment of our projects and plans."

"What is the swiftest and the slowest?" asked his interlocutor.

"Time," answered Zadig. "Nothing is more slow to him who expects, and nothing more swift to him who enjoys."

Salesman

Without a smiling face, do not become a merchant.

—*Chinese Proverb*

The Beauty of Old Age

The thought of old age sends a shudder through many hearts. But like most fears that beset us, this one is a lamentable delusion, and needless.

I looked long at the loveliness of a young cherry tree, a pink bouquet offered to the spirit of springtime. I thought no tree could be fairer, and sighed to think of the wanton breeze that would soon scatter the bloom and the beauty and leave to the tree but the dull duty of fruit-bearing.

Around the bend of the road there towered a noble tree, full two centuries old. It bore its majestic crown on a stem that rose like a bronze column reaching from earth to sky. It breathed a serenity, power, and understanding, and shed a great peace. The dainty pink tree was a poem, a lilting lyric poem; but this was an epic, a classic of majesty and music. Suddenly age meant something beyond all losing. It meant the gain of all that was good in life, kneaded into a soul that transcended all littleness, all trifling—a spirit aglow with an inner glory. Men are as trees walking.

"How beautiful you are!" exclaimed a young enthusiast to an old woman philosopher.

"My child, I ought to be beautiful. I have lived eighty years," she replied.

Youth is a time of fleeting beauty, a passage of storm and stress. We regret it, but we would not have it again if we might. Age brings peace; and it will, if we desire it, bring to us a beauty beyond the touch of the earth.—*Sunshine Magazine*

Everybody Has Problems

Perhaps it will ease the tension just to know that you aren't the only one who has troubles.

It has been pointed out that no one escapes problems. The details may differ but the problem that is bothering you this minute is probably also bothering thousands of other people across the country. When your children are terrible, 5,000 other children are becoming terrible, too. When your secretary loses something, 5,000 other secretaries are losing something at the same time. And when you are socking your golf ball into the creek, at least 5,000 other golfers are socking their golf balls into other creeks or lakes or rivers.

We all share a common humanity. Fate hasn't singled you out for rough treatment. Thousands of other people are experiencing the same frustrations, discouragements, and disappointments.

The next time you start feeling sorry for yourself just remember that you are not alone. Everybody has problems. —*Sunshine Magazine*

Comfort or Adventure

Parents should not over-emphasize comfort and security for their sons and daughters. A society in which the young people have lost their boldness and sense of adventure, is a society headed for the history book.—*John W. Gardner*

Character

I've never felt that football built character. That is done by parents and the church. You give us a boy with character and we'll give you back a man. You give us a character—and we'll give him right back to you.—*John McKay, Athletic Coach*

The Work You Did Today

Is anybody happier because you passed this way?
Does anyone remember that you spoke to him today?
This day is almost over, and its toiling time is through
Is there anyone to utter a kindly word of you?
Did you give a pleasant greeting to the friend who came along
Or a churlish sort of "howdy" and then vanish in the throng?
Were you selfish, pure and simple, as you rushed along your
way,
Or is someone mighty grateful for a deed you did today?

Can you say tonight in parting with the day that's slipping fast
That you helped a single brother of the many that you passed?
Is a single heart rejoicing over what you did or said?
Does a man whose hopes were fading now with courage look
ahead?
Did you waste the day or lose it, was it well or poorly spent?
Did you leave a trail of kindness or a scar of discontent?
As you close your eyes in slumber, do you think that God would
say
You have earned one more tomorrow by the work you did today?
—*Author Unknown, From Bulletin of Worden & Risberg*

Optimism

The fellow who talks about what a fool he used to be, certainly is an optimist.—*Arkansas Baptist*

That's the Trouble

Any baseball team could use a man who plays every position superbly, never strikes out and never makes an error; but there's no way to make him lay down his hot dog and come out of the grandstand.—*The Gourd, Eaton, Ohio Rotary Club*

Bible

The devil is not afraid of the Bible that has dust on it.

Safe Driving

Sign on a country road: "Drive carefully: there isn't a hospital within 50 miles."

Results

The world expects results. Don't tell others about the labor pains—show 'em the baby!—*Arnold H. Glasow*

Satire

Satire is one of the strongest weapons we have. The Satires of Juvenal changed the customs of Rome, Dean Swift changed the political aspect of England with his "Tale of a Tub," and Cervantes broke up the awful custom of Knight errantry in Spain by Don Quixote.

The Old Days

A few items from the first printed menu in America, offered patrons of Delmonico's in 1834. Bear in mind that this was an era when $1 a day was a man's top wage.

Tea or Coffee	1 cent
Soup	2 cents
Beef Stew	4 cents
Corn Beef and Cabbage	4 cents
Beef Steak	4 cents
Pork Chops	4 cents
Chicken Stew	5 cents
Roast Beef or Veal	5 cents
Ham and Eggs	10 cents
Roast Chicken	10 cents
½ Pie	2 cents

Regular Dinner — 12 cents

Don't Complain

Do you dread trips to the dentist? Be grateful for their modern skills and instruments and drugs. Before the advent of dentists, people went to blacksmiths to have their teeth fixed.

Our Heritage

The practical thing we can do, if we really want to make the world over again, is to try out the word "old" for a while. There are some "old" things that made this country.

There is the "old" virtue of religious faith.

There are the "old" virtues of complete integrity, loyalty, and truthfulness.

There is the "old" virtue of incorruptible service and honor in public office.

There are the "old" virtues of economy in government, of self-reliance, thrift, and individual liberty.

There are the "old" virtues of patriotism, real love of country, and willingness to sacrifice for it.

These "old" ideas are very inexpensive. They even would help win hot and cold wars. Some of these "old" things are slipping badly in American life. And if they slip too far, the lights will go out of America, even if we win the hot and cold wars. Think about it.—*Herbert Hoover*

The Month of May

Astronomers tell us that May has a dual personality—a gay, rejoicing one (Maypole dances and baskets) and a quiet understanding one (Mother's Day, Memorial Day). One of the many celebrations which combine these is at the battlefield of Valley Forge. Here one finds perhaps the most magnificent display of dogwood blossoms in the world, lying upon the hills like snowdrifts reflecting a sunset. Each Maytime at this national shrine—where heroes with bleeding feet once trod—200,000 Americans each year view the pink and white mingling of dogwood in flower—a commemoration of great beauty—a tribute to great bravery.—*Sunshine Magazine*

Values

Greatest handicap . . . Fear
Best day . . . Today
Greatest mistake . . . Giving up
Greatest stumbling block . . . Ego
Easiest to do . . . Find fault
Top comfort . . . Work well done
Greatest need . . . Common sense
Best gift . . . Forgiveness
Greatest knowledge . . . God
—*Weekly Progress, Marquette, Michigan*

A Short Course In Human Relations

This is a bit of philosophy on the use of words.
The six most important words: I admit I made a mistake.
The five most important words: You did a good job.
The four most important words: What is your opinion?
The three most important words: If you please—
The two most important words: Thank you!
The one most important word: We
The least important word: I

Lost and Alone

America is said to have the highest per capita boredom of any spot on earth! We know that because we have the greatest variety and greatest number of artificial amusements of any country. People have become so empty that they can't even entertain themselves. They have to pay other people to amuse them, to make them laugh, to try to make them feel warm and happy and comfortable for a few minutes, to try to lose that awful, frightening, hollow feeling—that terrible, dreaded feeling of being lost and alone.—*Billy Graham*

What a Simple Thing!

What a simple thing is a piece of iron with a coil of insulated wire around it! And yet, without that piece of iron and coil of wire we should today have no mammoth factories employing millions of men and women; there would be no huge powerhouses; no electric light, heat, or power; no telegraph and telephone systems of communication; no radio. The combination of the coil of wire and the core of iron forms what is known as the electromagnet—the most important industrial invention since the adoption of the wheel in ancient times.
—*Sunshine Magazine*

Living Philosophy

My own philosophy of life, as I reflect on its development, has gone through several stages—and, I hope, is continuing to grow. My parental and religious background gave me a somewhat undefined determination to serve God and my fellow man, but without any real plan to carry out this resolve.

During my first year out of college, while working for a steel company, I went through a period when I questioned seriously if I could achieve this goal in the business world. I thought, perhaps, I could serve more constructively in education, the church, or social work.

Wanting to share my doubts and seek advice, I confided in the personnel man who had hired me, whom I knew to be a thoughtful and religious man. He was generous with his time, and in our conversations he convinced me that a man could satisfy his ambition to serve God by working in any business or profession as long as it constructively serves society. My friend pointed out that a man can conduct his business affairs under Christian principles and ethics, and by his efforts serve his customers, his stockholders, his employees, his community and his God.

Ever since that day I have developed a firmer conviction that one can achieve his life's goal through any legitimate work he chooses, provided he loves his God and his neighbor, and makes that love manifest by the way he lives his life—inside and outside of his vocation.

From childhood, I had been familiar with the pronouncements of Jesus that one should love God with all his heart and soul and mind, and that he should love his neighbor as himself. But it was not until I was introduced to a small book entitled "The Greatest Thing in the World," by Henry Drummond, that I began really to comprehend these words.

In the 13th chapter of First Corinthians, St. Paul analyzed the real meaning of love, and Drummond interpreted his words in language I could understand—to give me a comprehensive guide for the conduct of my daily life. Paraphrasing the words of St. Paul, he said that love is made up of a spectrum of nine ingredients—each one a quality that, if achieved, would make up the stature of the perfect man. These nine ingredients are: Patience — kindness — generosity — humility — courtesy — unselfishness — good temper — guilelessness — and sincerity.

Being human, I frequently fail to live up to Jesus' commandments to love God and my neighbor, and I surely fall short of Drummond's analysis of love. But re-reading these words periodically helps to strengthen my resolve to follow them more carefully in the future. They are my conscience, and they prod me to serve God daily through my relationships with family and friends, and in my business, community and church activities.

I firmly believe that each of us as parents has a God-given opportunity to serve the world by providing our children with a home atmosphere of religion and love, by teaching them to accept responsibility for their own acts and the welfare of those less fortunate than they. One effective way to develop in our children a sense of responsibility to their community is for us, the parents, to participate in educational, church, charitable, political or similar activities for the betterment of our society.—*Talk delivered before the Chicago Sunday Evening Club, by Robert S. Ingersoll, Chairman and Chief Executive Officer, Borg-Warner Corporation*

Human Conduct

Prior to World War II, there was a general understanding in this country of what was appropriate conduct, of what were wise and proper limits of human behavior, of how people lived and worked together. There was no public confusion about these things. The North Star was firmly fixed in the North and if a person headed South, he knew it, and he knew that he was making himself an outcast.

Since World War II, there has been an ever-growing clamor to do away with the limits upon human conduct. The enthusiasts for thus "freeing" many are to be found in our schools and colleges, the public press, the news magazines, movies, novels and even the pulpit. Yes, religion, too, has been contaminated by this mounting stampede toward what is thought to be liberation. The church used to say, "Thou shalt" and "Thou shalt not." Now many clergymen are saying, "Well, let's have a discussion group," or "It's a matter of situational ethics" or "You should be guided by your own conscience."

Now let me offer some perspective. If you really use your brains, you will, I am confident, realize that the rise of civilization has been wholly dependent upon the development of institutionalized limits on human conduct. It is only as man has conceived and provided such agencies as law, religion, morality, patriotism and marriage, that people have been able to live in groups.—*From Commencement address by Dr. John A. Howard*

Challenges

Academic freedom is not an absolute. Like any other freedom, it is an ideal. Academic freedom is denatured as people use it as a cover to suppress the freedom of others to be heard.

A second misconception you will encounter in many colleges is that since college students are old enough to be drafted and get killed in wars, and old enough to have babies, the student should make his own decisions and the college should not in any way concern itself with the personal lives of the students. This is the basis on which one institution after another has been pressured into having "open" dormitories enabling the men students to visit in the women's bedrooms and vice versa, and pressured into tolerating the use of marijuana and hard drugs among the students.

Let me suggest to you that the student living under the protection of a college is not at all equivalent to the same person living in an apartment and holding a job. A student may go in heavy for drinking and miss four nine o'clock classes in a row with no great penalty. But the job-holder would suddenly become unemployed. A student may play revolutionary games through the SDS, or the Young Socialist Alliance, or the Red Guard, but he would think twice before he would thus jeopardize his job if he were working.

Actually, I don't think there is a college student in the country who wants the college to stop acting as a parent. Parents take care of their children financially until the child is able to care for himself.

Parents care for their young when they are sick or injured. From time to time I am called upon to decide whether to have an operation performed on a sick student when the parents are in Arabia or some place where they cannot be reached. This decision I make, in loco parentis. The college also stands in loco parentis when the students run afoul of the law. We bail them out when they do something stupid and we get them the best lawyers on the rare occasions when they have done something really bad, so that they have the full protection of the law.

This in loco parentis slogan has been used effectively and unscrupulously to coerce colleges into doing away with campus regulations concerning human conduct.

But that slogan has another vicious consequence. It implies that there is something bad about parents acting as parents when their sons and daughters reach college age and it thus reinforces a natural tendency of the college-age group to regard their parents as old-fashioned, rigid, unreasonable, heartless and a lot of other negative things.—*From a Commencement address by Dr. John A. Howard, President of Rockford College*

CHAPTER 3

USEFUL EXCERPTS FROM IMPORTANT SPEECHES

Health Care Costs

There are few subjects that touch on the lives of everyone in America. The theme of my remarks today is one of them. Along with the age-old question about "What can we do about the weather?" one of the few matters that concerns everyone is health. While little has been done so far to improve the weather outdoors . . . and therefore its cost has been little affected . . . a great deal has been done about health and as new scientific knowledge in medicine is developed and applied, costs appear that never existed before.

So now we have the question what to do about the cost of health care because in our lifetime we have come from where the practice of medicine consisted mostly of a hopeful and concerned physician with a few effective drugs and some nostrums . . . to an extremely complex profession capable of dealing with scores of diseases, of performing heart transplants, and with a great explosion of new knowledge and techniques.

Health care costs are going to continue to rise. However, so will the quality of care provided by the physician to his patients continue to go up. More can be done by the physician for his patients today than ever before. This is largely due to continuing improvements in his training and his ongoing interest in updating his medical knowledge and the knowledge available. Continuing medical education is a lifelong process with most American physicians.

The steadily increasing sophistication of health care in the United States has resulted in the virtual elimination of some diseases . . . and there will be continued progress in the field of preventive medicine. But greater physician skills and new techniques require the assistance of more highly trained technicians and the use of costlier equipment.

Nevertheless, increasing health care costs are frequently offset by shorter time away from the wage earner's job, and by saving of productive lives which would not have been possible, in some instances, as recently as ten years ago or less.

Health care costs not only have become important because so very much more can be done for so many more people . . . but it is wrapped up in the strongest emotions of man. For life and death . . . or at least health and well-being . . . are involved.

The sick person, or the parent of the sick child, is worried and often distraught when in need of medical help. All fears and resentments are magnified. Then, when the illness is over and pushed out of mind, the bills come in. This requires payment for services people wish they did not need and that usually are unplanned for.

When people know they are benefiting from increasingly expensive physical facilities and equipment, and from highly sophisticated personnel and services, they are quite willing to pay for them. For example, intensive-care or coronary care units often have hospital charges from $75 to $125 or even more a day—but because people can see how much is involved in them, they accept the need for such costs, as do insurance carriers.

When a person passively submits to diagnostic tests, he is not aware of the substantial laboratories, the highly skilled personnel, the costly and often rapidly obsolescent equipment involved behind the scene.

He does not realize what a complex, manpower-demanding entity a modern hospital is with 2.65 employees for every patient and special services available 24 hours a day and on weekends and holidays. He thinks of it as a sort of hotel with "quiet" signs. So he doesn't understand why bills are so much larger than they used to be when few tests were known and few services were provided.—*Dr. Dwight Wilbur, Former President, American Medical Association*

My Philosophy

A philosophy must have several facets. I will try to divide mine into three categories—my attitude toward God, my attitude toward myself, and my attitude toward others.

First, I have a growing faith and belief in God. I believe that as a creation of God, I can depend on Him for all the spiritual and moral strength that I need, all the guidance that I must have, and all the intelligence that I require to make the right decisions.

I firmly believe that God reveals Himself as man diligently searches. I believe that we are continually rediscovering God and that God shows Himself to us in the teachings of Jesus Christ as well as in numerous other ways. I believe that the Bible gives us guidance for the programming of our daily living.

I believe that God continues to create, that the universe is evolving and that man is evolving. Scientific study and research as well as such programs as the recent space flights constantly reveal additional wonders of the universe, and man is challenged by the discoveries that have been made to find more of the meaning of life and God.

For the second facet—my attitude toward myself, I believe that God has endowed me with certain talents. They are different than the talents that have been given to any other single person. I believe that I must employ to the fullest extent possible the talents that have been given to me. I feel that if I do not do so, I will not have fulfilled my rightful destiny and that I will be basically an unhappy person.

In developing my talents, I have found that I must seek learning with a passion. This at times has required a sacrifice in order to obtain knowledge. I firmly believe that learning should not be pursued for the sake of knowledge itself, but in order to serve others better.

Lastly, as to my attitude toward others, I employ a variant of the golden rule which, as we all know, provides "Do unto others as you would have them do unto you." My variant is "When dealing with another, try to place yourself in his shoes and act accordingly."

This has not been an easy thing for me to do. It has not come naturally. It has required a lot of patience. And I have not always succeeded. But I believe that this is the mark of a mature person. If the rule were followed universally, I am sure that we would not have the conflicts that we have today in our society—the problems of law and order—the hostilities among nations.

These three facets are the essence of my living philosophy. Each of you has one also. I would like to suggest that each of you sit down and write out yours—and you will be a better person for having done it. —*Given before the Chicago Sunday Evening Club, by James Coultrap, Chairman of the Board, Miehle-Goss-Dexter, Incorporated*

Go All the Way

One of my daughters loves animals, and we've been through the parakeet and poodle and cat and gerbil and hamster and white mice and on-and-on business, but we hadn't gotten around to the tropical fish thing. We finally decided the time had come for tropical fish. There's quite a bit to this business of tropical fish I hadn't realized before. After you get into the store they talk you into about thirty or forty dollars worth of equipment. Of course, you've got to have the filters and the pumps and all the rest of it. We also found, for example, that the $2.95 fish eat up the fifty-cent fish. This is part of the deal I didn't know about before. Then the man told us you have to have a $1.50 scavenger fish. This was absolutely necessary, so we bought a $1.50 scavenger fish. Then the first thing he scavenged and ate up was a $1.50 plant we had put in the aquarium, so this made him worth $3.00 and we had no plant.

On one of our visits back to the store a little kid came in and started bothering the man, asking what he could buy for ten cents, and finally the man said, "I'll sell you one guppie for ten cents." We were laughing at this interplay, and he said, "Don't laugh." He said, "There was some little kid in here the other day and I gave him a guppie, and it ended up costing his father $85.00 because he brought his father back, and they bought the thirty-gallon tank, the pumps, the filters, the whole business." My first thought was, that clerk is really sharp. When you can parlay a guppie into an $85.00 sale he's really got something going. But my admiration is much more for that father. Now I realize, not many of us have $85.00 to spend on fish tanks. That's not the point. But I said to myself afterwards, if you're going to go in for raising guppies with your boy, then go all the way, and that's precisely what this father had done. And I thought to myself, how few people really can do this, really, in the name and in the spirit of God, to go all the way, to give themselves to whatever they're doing, to live life to the hilt.—*The Reverend Edward W. Bauman*

The First Talking Pictures

Everyone had to sing in the pictures. My first picture was called, "Smiling Irish Eyes," and I was supposed to sing, "Come Back to Erin, Mavourneen, Mavourneen." Now you know even Galli Curci had trouble with that one.

I had singing lessons, but I came from a family that is noted for singing off key, and I worst of all. Now the hundred-piece orchestra couldn't drown me out. They tried everything, and finally the director hit upon an idea. He said, "Look—your lover is in New York and you're sad because he's away from you. So just burst out crying, and you can go off key all the way and it won't be noticed." That's the way we did it and it really came out fine.—*Colleen Moore*

The 1930s

As our beloved friend whom we all know, John Barriger, great historian—great railroad man—as he said about the history of the 1930s, "First the banks liquidated their customers who promptly returned the compliment."—*Eliot Janeway*

All About Mary Pickford

Mary Pickford was one of our most loved people, and rightly so. She and Douglas were the idols of all the young people. The thing we longed for most in all the world was to get an invitation to dinner to Pickfair, because they entertained the royalty.

I remember when Lord and Lady Mountbatten, who were the leaders of the beautiful people of the Twenties, spent part of their honeymoon there; and then the Duke of Alba came, and even Marconi. The place was always filled with the famous of the world; and when they came to California they only wanted to see two people, Mary and Doug.

Mary's real name was Gladys Schmitt, and she was born in Toronto, Ontario. One time Mary and Doug were entertaining the King and Queen of Siam, and they were playing tennis. It had rained the day before, and the little Queen slipped off the tennis court into a mud puddle. So Mary picked her up and took her into the house; gave her some fresh clothes; went into the bathroom; turned the water on in the tub, and Mary said, as she came out—she leaned against the wall, "Imagine you, Gladys Schmitt, of Toronto, Ontario, with the Queen of Siam in her bathtub."—*Colleen Moore*

Easy Way Out

Many of us seem preoccupied today with getting through life without serious involvement. I am not talking here about those dramatic or horrifying cases in which people turn their backs when they see or hear fellow human beings in desperate trouble. I am talking about those little things which are a clue toward the national attitude.

We swaddle our babies in disposable diapers, we drink sugar-free soda pop from throw-away bottles, we patronize painless dentists, and, on formal occasions, we wear clip-on ties. We search for and then rely on easy payments, same day credit, precooked foods, even instant religion, thanks to Dial-A-Prayer. But the things which are supposed to make life so easy are but symptoms of the new age of noninvolvement.

Many of us today wish for things we'd like to have, but seek to avoid the price.—*Stephen B. Labunski*

Choose You This Day

This brings me to the end of my talk to you on the subject of education. It has been a real pleasure to be allowed to talk to such a distinguished gathering.

I suggest to you that when all things are said and done, one great fact, the greatest fact, remains supreme and unassailable. It is this.

There are in this world things that are true and things that are false; there are ways that are right and ways that are wrong; there are men good, and men bad. And on one side or the other we must take our stand; one, or the other, we must serve.

I am a soldier and I would like to remind you that a great commander once dismissed his troops after a long campaign with these words:

"Choose you this day who ye will serve; as for me and my house, we will serve the Lord."
Joshua 24, verse 15

Those are great words by Joshua.

Should they not be impressed on every boy during the vital formative years? And are not these words the foundation of the whole matter?—*Field Marshal Viscount Montgomery*

A Hoosier Speaks

We're living in days of confusion. These are days, you know, when a girl wears curlers to the wedding so she'll look nice for the reception.

We're as confused as one of our oldtime speakers here, Gene Flack, once said, about the two boys fighting in Hollywood. One said, "My dad can whip your dad."

The other one said, "Why, your dad is my dad!"

Then we even went to things so strange as the boy who killed his father and mother, and then put himself on the mercy of the court because he was an orphan.

I had one the other day that wrote me, and he said, "I'd like to come down to your office and sit across the desk from you and spit in your face."

"Well," I said, "come on, if your aim isn't any better than your manners you can't hit me."

Because of these current complexities I thought it was not inappropriate to discuss Indiana a little bit—its lessons, its people; its philosophy.

Of course, you have to start out with Thomas Riley Marshall, our distinguished Vice President and once Governor of the State, who said Indiana had produced more first-class second-rate men than any State in the Union.

Where else could such immortal sentiments be born?

He also said when someone asked him one time, "Do you think that paying higher salaries would get better judges in Indiana?"

He said, "No, just more applicants!"

He said another thing that politicians should well remember and that is that a free dinner may be the most expensive one you ever ate.

He also said something that always impressed me when I get frightened about people threatening me, and he said, "You can't scare a man about falling out of bed when he's already sleeping on the floor."—*Roger D. Branigin, Former Governor of Indiana*

Time Savers

There is a great demand for automatic appliances that turn themselves on and off, and even do a series of operations without attention, so that the housewife can be spending her valuable time doing something else.

The desire for more leisure time is so strong that saving minutes, and even seconds, has become an important goal for all of us. The word "instant" is sheer magic, and offsets many deficiencies in other product qualities. Your car must start with the turn of the switch. Parking takes time, which you won't take. So, you patronize the supermarket with plenty of parking space, the drive-in movie, the drive-in lunchroom, the drive-in bank, and even the drive-in hotel, which is usually known as a motel.

You want your rented car waiting for you when you arrive at the airport, and you criticize the airline, which saved you twenty hours of travel time, because you have to wait ten minutes for your baggage. Even when you take your family out for a destinationless ride on a spring Sunday afternoon and have to stop for gasoline, you resent the time the service station attendant takes to clean your windshield and check your oil.

Your bread is presliced, your coffee is instant, and the rest of your meal requires no time for preparation of the food for cooking and, in many cases today, is largely precooked. To save still more valuable time, your wife can now take a packaged dinner out of the freezer, pop it into the oven, and serve it to you in the original foil container, which she throws away after dinner without having to take the time to wash the plate.

You read your novels abridged, your articles digested, your magazines in pictures, and your newspapers in tabloid size, just to save time. About the only written words that people haven't been able to condense are the Ten Commandments.

We can come to only one conclusion. As long as anything we do or use takes any time at all, and as long as people have the desire for more leisure time to do more things they think they will enjoy, there are opportunities for smart people to gain an advantage by selling the luxury of time-saving. And so it is with the luxury of ease—the saving of effort. No matter how industrious we are, we all have our share of laziness.

The thousands of people who have invented new kinds of can openers may have been crazy, but they weren't stupid. Maybe no one will ever invent a good one, but we WILL have packages that are easy to open.—*Jervis J. Babb*

A Disciple

You know, of course, that the policy of the Communist is single-minded, to be just a disciple, a zealot for his religion. And the religion of Communism is that there is no God, and Karl Marx is his prophet.—*Rabbi Charles E. Shulman*

Marketing Today

The things you and your family buy must be ready to use and require the absolute minimum of physical effort. Try and sell a product today with a label on it, "Shake Well Before Using!" Cream may look nice and rich on top of the milk, but most folks would rather have it homogenized. Sliced cheese is preferred to brick cheese, but cheese spreads are even easier, and many folks aren't bothered at all that they don't even taste like cheese. Tea may be better made in the pot, but it's less trouble to drop a teabag in the cup.

And so it goes. Little bits of effort saved, like lowering your bread automatically in the toaster and popping up the next Kleenex when you pull the first one, may easily make the difference between being the leader in a business or having to work harder to make a living. As we have just seen, we are all vitally interested in saving effort and conserving our strength.—*Jervis J. Babb*

His Favorite Translation

Three men were talking about some of the recent translations of the Bible. One said, "I like that Phillips version of the Gospels. It's easy reading. The Revised isn't bad either."

"Maybe," the second man shrugged his shoulder. "But, believe me, nothing compares to the King James version."

"I know a better one," said the third man.

"What do you mean?"

"I like my mother's translation best. She translated the Bible into life, and it was the most convincing translation I ever saw."

Cynicism

Too many Americans out of our teeming millions have adopted cynicism as a philosophy of life. Individuals who follow that pattern are indifferent to their neighbors. They are indifferent to their civic duties. They won't vote unless the sun is shining. They are indifferent to public service. They are indifferent to their own religion. They are indifferent to the world situation; let the nations of the world be damned, so long as they have their income and their means and their pleasures.

For such people as these, one clergyman by the name of Ziegler, of Roanoke, Virginia, recently wrote a re-do of the 23rd Psalm that bears repetition, indicating the American love of gadgetry and worship of the machine. Let me quote it to you.

"Science is my shepherd; I shall not want.

He maketh me to lie down on foam rubber mattresses,

He leadeth me beside six-lane highways.

He rejuveneth my thyroid gland.

He leadeth me in the paths of psychoanalysis, for peace of mind's sake.

Yea, though I walk through the valley of the shadow of the Iron Curtain, I will fear no Communist, for thou art with me.

Thou preparest a banquet for me, in the presence of the world's billion hungry people.

Thou annointest my head with home permanents.

Surely, prosperity and pleasure shall follow me all the days of my life, and I shall dwell in Shangri-la forever."

These are bitter lines, written by a clergyman as a take-off, as a parody of something of what is going on in our modern day, if we care to face it.—*Rabbi Charles E. Shulman*

Materialism

If we accept the concept of materialism, quantitative things, we have ample warnings from our poets as to what is going to happen, because they are usually ahead of our time. Let me remind you about one of them, a great and famous man, Stephen Vincent Benet, who died too young in our nation. He wrote a little piece called "Nightmare with the Angels.'" I am only quoting a few lines. Here is what he says:

"You will not be saved by General Motors.
You will not be saved by prefabricated houses.
You will not be saved by dialetic materialism.
You will not be saved by the Lambeth Conference.
You will not be saved by Vitamin D.
You will not be saved by the expanding universe.
In fact, you will not be saved."

—*Rabbi Charles E. Shulman*

Encourages Checkups

When you go to your doctor for a checkup I hope you understand the rationale. Most people have the notion that they come to us so we can pick up some fatal disease in time to nip it in the bud. This does happen—but very rarely. Most people don't have more than one fatal disease in their whole lifetime!

The principal reason for having a physical examination is to determine that you are healthy, so that you can plunge into your exercise and work without fear of straining some damaged organ, and to get some advice upon which of your bad habits to modify in order to extend your life.

Unfortunately I find that most people who come to me for this service aren't particularly interested in being told which bad habits to give up. They want to know which ones they can hang on to for at least one more year.—*Dr. Richard C. Bates*

Compare Today's Expectancy With Yesteryear's

In the last fifty years we have finally identified a few factors that help to determine the age at which a man dies.

As you know, about five years ago we finally achieved for the average person in this country the Biblical promise of three score years and ten, or 70 years of life expectancy. In 1900, the average life expectancy at birth in this country was but 47 years.

Unfortunately this cannot be taken to mean that you and I are going to live 23 years longer than our grandparents, because once one has arrived at the age of fifty, his life expectancy is only four years longer than it would have been had he been fifty in 1900.

Even in Biblical times it was recognized that three score years and ten, or 70, is a good average life span. This tremendous rise in life expectancy in the past seventy years is almost entirely a reflection of the elimination of the great childhood epidemics of yesteryear.

A hundred years ago a quarter of our infants failed to survive the first year of life, and, of course, when one has a large infant mortality it drops the life expectancy average considerably. Once one survives infancy he isn't living much longer than man has ever lived.

There is for every species of animal some preset life expectancy, the mechanisms for which are entirely unknown. A rat is old at three; a dog at 15; an elephant at 50. Man is the longest lived of all animals at 80.

If you leave animals, turtles are known to live to the age of 200—if you can call what a turtle does living.—*Dr. Richard C. Bates*

Crime

Society's problem with those who will not obey law has never loomed so large in our national life as it does today.

People murder others in this country at the rate of more than one for every hour of the day.

There are more than 140 crimes of theft every hour; assault and violence and rape grow comparably.

The murder rate is 10,000 human lives a year, which is higher than the death rate in our current military operations in Vietnam which inspire such emotional and violent public demonstrations.

And the growth rate of crime is now far greater than the growth in our population.

Perhaps the most alarming thing is the large amount of crime committed by persons under age 20, which suggests that homes, parents, schools, churches and communities have somewhere failed.

Even worse is the fact that the highest rate of repeaters—recidivists—is in this under-20 age bracket. Nearly 60 percent of the 20-and-under are repeaters.—*Judge Warren E. Burger of the U. S. Supreme Court, Washington, D. C.*

Serving Others

Every instinct, starting with self-preservation, is for man to serve himself. But over the ages he has surrendered, consciously or not, to the knowledge that all the pressures of civilization are joined in a single requirement; that if he is to serve himself best, he must serve others well.

This principle is fundamental to man's ability to coexist peacefully and productively. His awareness of this principle predates all the great religions. Consider, if you will, the way in which the basic idea is repeated in each of them.

Judaism: "What is hateful to you, do not to your fellow man."

Islam: "No one of you is a believer until he desires for his brother that which he desires for himself."

Hinduism: "This is the sum of duty: Do naught unto others which could cause you pain if done to you."

Buddhism: "Hurt not others in ways that you yourself would find hurtful."

Confucianism: "Do not unto others what you would not have them do unto you."

Christianity's "Golden Rule," then, is a repetition of what man, everywhere, and in all ages, has agreed was a maxim to be followed for life.—*William S. Beinecke, Chairman, The Sperry & Hutchinson Company*

Indiana

Indiana is a little over one hundred and fifty years old.

We are—we were once a part of the proud Province of Virginia, and the second state carved from the Northwest Territory; it is the smallest one—38,000 square miles. It stretches from the First Principal Meridian, which is the Ohio State Line to the Wabash River, and from the dams of the Ohio to the Dunes of Illinois.

Here five million people live in continual political discord, but en masse bearing a distinct flavor as Hoosiers. None, even Texans, are as fiercely proud of their heritage as those of us who call ourselves Hoosiers.

Our history has been a series of lessons, some of which we have adhered to and some which we have not, in war; in finance; in communism; in literature; and in politics.

The first Hoosier, and our first lesson, was brought to us by George Rogers Clark—that intrepid Virginia redhead, who knew the Muskingum and the Kanawha, and who, it says, was sent out here by Wythe, Harrison, and Patrick Henry to organize the militia, but actually to settle Kaskaskia, Cahokia and Vincennes.

They promised him $20,000. They actually gave him and his men a hundred thousand acres of land across from Louisville on Silver Creek. This is almost like a country woman giving away rhubarb.

It took a commission nineteen years to divide that land. They gave 2400 acres to a captain, and on down to 40 acres to a private, which is about the same distribution we have in any conflict that the Hoosier State has been involved in.

Virginia gave him a sword instead of money, and he stuck it in the ground at Clarksville, broke off the hilt and threw it into the Ohio River. Then he proceeded to get drunk before the fire.

With a bullet in his teeth, and no anaesthesia his left leg was amputated, to the music of a fife and a drum. There are some lessons there, if you would but heed them . . .

George Rogers Clark we see again in other Hoosiers. History repeats itself, but not so often as historians repeat each other.—*Roger D. Branigin, the Governor of Indiana*

CHAPTER 4

HUMOROUS STORIES

He Better Like It

"There you are, dear," said the wife, putting the plate before her husband. "Cooked just the way you'd better like it."

The Cause

You perhaps know of the great confrontation between big, fat Gilbert K. Chesterton and little, skinny Bernard Shaw; and Chesterton looked at Shaw and said, "Man, you look like a famine!" And Shaw said, "Yeah, you look as if you caused it!"—*Dr. John Rock*

Not So Good

An American astronaut was poised in his capsule, ready to be launched. A reporter asked: "How do you feel?"

"How would you feel," the astronaut replied, "if you were sitting on top of 150,000 parts—each supplied by the lowest bidder?"

Don't Worry

Young man: "Darling, I'm ruined. I lost my job. I'm bankrupt. I haven't a cent."

Sweet young thing: "Don't worry, sweetheart, I'll always love you—even if I never see you again."

Nothing Wrong

A small boy was standing near the escalator in a department store watching the moving handrail.

"Something wrong?" asked the clerk.

"Nope," said the lad, "just waiting for my chewing gum to come back."

Correct Subject?

At a recent women's club meeting, it was estimated that 20% wore rouge, 35% of those present tinted their hair, 75% plucked their eyebrows, 80% had permanent waves, 85% wore eyeshadow, 90% wore fingernail polish, 100% used lipstick, and 10% wore false eyelashes and other cosmetic camouflage. Their subject for discussion: "Deceptive Packaging."—*Program Notes*

Not Painless

Johnny: "The dentist you sent me to wasn't really painless."

Mom: "Why, darling, did he hurt you?"

Johnny: "No, but I bit his finger, and he yelled."

He Had Her There

Said the wife, gently, "You've got your hat on backwards again."

Her professor husband replied testily, "What do you mean backwards? How do you know which way I intend to go?"

He Will Succeed

After the college boy delivered the telegram the man at the door asked, "What is the usual tip for a delivery?"

"Well," replied the youth, "this is my first trip here, but the other fellows said that if I get a dime out of you, I'm doing great."

"Is that so?" snorted the man. "Well, just to show them how wrong they are, here's a dollar."

"Thanks," replied the messenger. "I'll put this into my special school fund."

"What are you studying?" asked the man.

The lad smiled, "Applied psychology, sir."

Sure Sign

They were hunting elephants on safari along the grassy banks of a small river. One of the hopeful new hunters turned to the guide.

"How will we detect the presence of an elephant?" he asked.

The guide whispered, "By the faint odor of peanuts on his breath."

Modern

A mother was shopping for a toy for her young son. The manager of the local department store offered a put-it-together-yourself toy which she considered much too complicated.

"But you have missed the point, madam," the manager said. "This toy is designed to teach the young the realities of our confused time and has the approval of the best authorities on child raising. No matter how your child puts the toy together, it won't work."

Wrong Guess

While participating in Parents' Day at a local college, two visitors noticed a couple of flower children walking across the campus.

"I wonder if they're girls or boys?" mused the wife.

To satisfy his wife's curiosity, the husband shuffled over to the pair and asked, "Are you two sisters?"

"Sisters?" the cute one with the cigar replied. "Man, we're not even Catholics."

Was That Nice?

A young wife just learning to drive had succeeded in completely snarling traffic. Excited she turned to her husband and asked what to do.

"I don't know," he replied calmly, "but I'm sure if you climb into the back seat you can figure it out."

How About Blue?

Her car stalled at the corner, and the traffic light kept changing—red, yellow, green, red, yellow, green.

The policeman stepped over to the car and asked in a hurt voice: "What's the matter, lady, ain't we got any colors you like?"

Getting to the Top

There are two ways of reaching the top of an oak tree. One is to climb it. Of course the other is to sit on an acorn. I wouldn't advise either.—*Dr. John Rock*

Nuthin' to It

Tommy, the football enthusiast, said to his little sister, "Well, we won the game, nuthin' to nuthin'."

"Who made the first nuthin'? she asked.

An Old Favorite

Mother: "What did you do at the party?"
Little Laura: "We sang the refrigerator song."
Mother: "How does that go?"
Little Laura: "Freeze a jolly good fellow . . ."

Playing Safe

After saying his usual night prayers, Johnny was heard bawling out this petition:

"Dear Lord, I pray that I will get a new bicycle for Christmas and an electric train, if it isn't too much!"

"What are you shouting for?" asked his little brother. "God isn't deaf."

"I know," said Johnny, "but Grandma is."

Observant

Sunday school teacher: Willie, do you know what becomes of little boys who use bad language, when they're playing marbles?

Willie: Yes, sir. They grow up and play golf.

Frank

Booked for surgery, a businessman filled out the hospital questionnaire this way: Q—Who will pay your bill? A—Wife. Q—Relationship? A—Hostile.

Unlucky

Joe: My wife dreamed last night she was married to a millionaire.

Jack: You're lucky. Mine thinks that in the daytime.

He Knew

"I don't feel good, mamma," said the little boy.

"I'm sorry. Where do you feel worse?" asked his mother solicitously.

"In school, mama."

Qualified

An ignorant precinct worker announced to his ward boss that in reward for his door bell pulling activities for the party, he wanted to be made postmaster of his town.

"No, that kind of a job isn't for you," the boss said. "Why, you can't read and write."

"I don't want to be assistant postmaster," the guy replied. "I want to be postmaster."

Is That Nice?

A golfer, trying to get out of a trap, said, "The traps on this course are annoying, aren't they?"

"Yes," said the second golfer, trying to putt, "would you mind closing yours?"

More Effective

"Glad to see you getting to school on time these mornings," said the teacher.

"Yes, sir, I've got a parrot now," said the student.

"A parrot! Why not an alarm clock?"

"I never seem to hear alarm clocks," explained the youth. "But now I've got this parrot. And what the parrot says when the alarm wakes him up is enough to wake up anybody."

Is This Clear

Overheard in the department store exchange line, one lady to another: "Oh, I loved it, frankly, but you know what bad taste I have."

Strict Traffic Rules

A man was leading a flock of sheep down the main street of a small village when he was ordered to halt by the town constable.

"What's wrong?" the sheep herder asked. "I have a small flock of ewes, and I was just going to turn off onto a side street."

"That's the trouble," the constable replied. "No ewe turns are permitted on Main Street in this town."

No Picnic

(Lady entering bus with twelve children)
Bus driver: Are they all yours or is this a picnic?
Lady: They're all mine and it's no picnic.

Good While It Lasted

A man was applying for employment with a certain industry and asked the personnel manager: "Does your company pay my Blue Cross insurance?"

"No, you pay for it; it's deducted from your salary each month," he was informed.

"Last place I worked they paid for it," the applicant said.

"Did they give you a life insurance policy, too?" the interviewer asked.

"Sure."

"Profit sharing?"

"Sure."

"Two and three-week vacations?"

"Yes, and they had big bonuses, and gifts for your birthday, and —"

"Why did you leave?"

"The company folded."

Progress

It was quite an important preview of a new film adapted from a novel by a very popular writer. Afterwards he was asked what he thought of it. "Excellent," he replied. "Who wrote the story?" "You did," was the answer. "We got it from your book."

"I wouldn't have known it," said the author. "But it would make an excellent novel. Mind if I use it?"

"Of course not," came the reply, "so long as you give us an option on the film rights."

Taking Care of Himself

The four-year-old daughter of a friend of mine was accustomed to pray for everyone in a rather large family. She always concluded, "Please bless Daddy and Mommy and Jimmy."

One evening before she could finish, Jimmy, her five-year-old brother, who was kneeling beside her, became tired of so much blessing. "Don't bless me, I'll bless myself," he said and began his own brief prayer.—*Annie Laurie Von Tungeln, Parents' Magazine*

She Knew That

A bebopper's wife, concerned about his behavior, coaxed him into seeing a psychiatrist. After an hour with the patient, the doctor emerged from his office and said, "Madam, I must tell you that your husband is crazy."

"I know that," said the wife. "But what's wrong with him?"

Stars Everywhere

President Eisenhower's favorite story:

It is about the time he landed in Africa. His shoes didn't. fit. It was raining cats and dogs, so he slipped on a raincoat and put another over his head like a cape and went to the tent where a sergeant was issuing shoes. Ike had a slip with the right size shoes marked on it and handed it to the sergeant.

The sergeant could not tell the rank of the rain-soaked applicant. Cigarette in mouth, the sergeant came back with a shoe in either hand just as Ike, with rain running down his neck, threw back the rain cape. The sergeant, taking one look at all those stars, dropped cigarette and shoes as he exclaimed, "Holy smoke, it's the milky way!"—*Boston Globe*

Optimists and Pessimists

A German, visiting Paris, was idly passing the time at a street cafe with a French acquaintance. Asked how they determined the difference between an optimist and a pessimist in Germany, he replied: "Ach! That is easy. The optimists are all learning to speak English, while the pessimists are learning Russian."

A Mighty Drive

A Londoner visiting St. Andrews for the first time determined to try a round of golf. Furnishing himself with the usual implements and caddie, he went out before breakfast.

It seemed quite easy, and his first drive was a terrific swipe. When the turf had ceased to decend he turned, somewhat dazed, to the caddie and asked: "What did I hit just now, my lad?"

Came the reply: "Scotland, sir."

Stories of Jimmy Durante

"I goes into the Automat and puts a lead nickel in da slot. And what do you think comes out? The MANAGER!"

"I'm lyin' on the park bench takin' my siesta—as is my wont—when along comes a bunch of flies and settles of my nose. I lets 'em loiter—live and let live is my motter. Den a bee comes along, lights on my nose and stings me. 'Dat does it!' I says, 'Dere's always gotta be a smart aleck in every crowd. Now—just for that—EVERYBODY OFF.' "

"I buys a new convertible. I'm exubilent. Watta car. I push a button. The top stays where it is—but the bottom falls out."

"A guy tells me, 'Hey, Jimmy, there's a fly on the end of your nose. Why don't you brush it off?' 'You brush it off,' I tells him. 'It's closer to you dan it is ta me.' "

Modern Children

Modern mother to neighbor: "I always wanted a child with long hair, but I was hoping it would be a girl."

Can It Vote

On a trip to the far west former Vice President Humphrey was shown a power pump that a plant manager proudly told him had replaced 200 workers.

"That's fine," said Humphrey, "but can it vote?"

Looking Ahead

James A. Farley, former postmaster general reports that a well-known New York broker ordered his chauffeur to stop at an insane asylum every morning so that he could watch an inmate pitching baseball. A friend was puzzled by the daily ritual and asked the broker why he stopped at the same asylum every day to watch the same pitcher.

"It's like this," said the broker, "if things go on the way they are, someday I'll be in there catching for him and I want to study his curves."

Slow Down

In this day of air travel, it is hard to believe some of the quaint laws that used to regulate railroads. A law of one community read: "It is against the law for a train to enter the city limits unless preceded by a man on horseback."

Absolutely Sure

He: "Then it's all set. We elope at midnight?"

She: "Yes, darling."

He: "Are you sure you have everything packed in your suitcase?"

She: "I'm positive. Papa and mamma helped me."

Practical Viewpoint

"Give me an example of unremunerative outlay of capital," said the professor of political economy.

While the star students hesitated, a young man at the back of the room suggested: "Taking your sister out on a date."

Right Answer

Little Helga, aged five, was the daughter of Norwegian parents who had come to America shortly before she was born. When Helga went to Sunday School the first time, the teacher asked what nationality her name stood for. Helga tossed her flaxen curls and replied with dignity: "I'm an American of Norwegian design."

Open House—Modern Jail

Sheriff Joseph D. Lohman
and the Chaplains of the Cook County Jail
Request the Honor of Your Company
at an
OPEN HOUSE
Introducing the Newly Remodeled Chapel
Cook County Jail
26th Street and California Avenue
Chicago, Illinois

Cooperation

The Little Leaguer put all his sixty pounds into a ferocious swing and connected—barely. The ball scraped by the bottom of the bat, jiggled straight back to the pitcher, who groped and fumbled it. There was still plenty of time to nail the batter at first, but the pitcher's throw soared high over the first baseman's head. The slugger flew on toward second base. Somebody retrieved the ball. The next throw sailed into left field wildly.

The hitter swaggered into third, puffing through a man-sized grin, then continued on to cross the final plate.

"Oh, boy!" he said. "That's the first home run I ever hit in my whole life!"

The Big One Got Away

If a fisherman fibs to us,
Is his fib amphibious?

It Is Difficult

As they window-shopped at the furniture store, the new bride said to her husband, "I just cannot see how they make all that nice walnut furniture out of those crinkly little old walnuts."

Smart Boy

Mother and daughter were in the kitchen washing dishes while father and seven-year-old Johnny were in the living room. Suddenly father and son heard a crash of falling dishes. They listened expectantly.

"It was Mom," said Johnny.

"How do you know?" asked his father.

"Because," answered Johnny, "she isn't saying anything."

Seems Probable

"Was it while you were on the football team that you were hurt?" asked the doctor.

"No, sir," replied the limping player. "It was when the football team was on me."

Speed Reading

Bill: "Why did you spend so much to learn speed reading?"

Jack: "My boy, when you drive the expressways like I do, you read fast or you never get off."

Then You Are OK

A man about to go on a vacation to Mexico asked his druggist, who had recently returned from a short visit, whether he had any advice on how not to get sick down there. His counsel was: "First, don't drink the water. And second, don't eat the food."

Looking Ahead

Two small boys were playing together when a very pretty little girl walked by. One of the boys said fervently to his pal, "Boy, when I stop hating girls, she's the one I'll stop hating first!"

Uses His Noodle

The mouse of the house lives a life of ease, his food problem is just a snap; he has cleverly learned now to nibble the cheese without ever springing the trap.

She Knew the Answer

A woman on a television audience-participation show was asked the name of her favorite author.

"Why, it's my husband," she replied.

"Your husband?" questioned the interviewer: "What does he write that you particularly like?"

The woman smiled brightly, then answered: "Checks."

Next Question?

Two fish were swimming along together in the river when the little fish asked the much larger fish: "How did you manage to grow so big?"

"My friend," he replied, "when I was about your size I learned to keep my mouth shut, so here I am."

The Solution

Jenson: "You say you're not bothered any more with relatives coming and staying? How did you do it?"

Benson: "It was easy. I borrowed from the rich ones and lent it to the poor ones, and none of them came back."

Manners

The other day in a restaurant I saw a man with such poor manners he was actually scratching his back with his fork. I got so upset at seeing this I dropped a handful of mashed potatoes.

Age

If your first love letter had a five-cent stamp, you're still young. If it had a four-cent stamp, you're middle-aged. If it had a two-cent stamp, you're Gramps.

They Certainly Aren't

Little Johnny was second in his class, and the top place was held by a girl.

"Surely, Son," said his father, "you are not going to let yourself be beaten by a mere girl."

"Well, you see, Daddy," Johnny explained soberly, "girls aren't nearly as mere as they used to be."

Taxes

The pioneers would have shed big tears and thrown away their axes, if in a dream they'd caught a gleam of what we pay in taxes!

It Could Be

Two small boys were out hunting in the woods and one of them stopped to pick up a chestnut burr. "Hey, Tom!" he called. "Come here, I've found a porcupine egg!"

It Certainly Was

Professor: "Didn't you have a brother in this class last semester?"

Student: "No, sir. It was I. I'm taking the course over."

Professor: "Extraordinary resemblance, though . . . extraordinary."

Clear Instructions

Bill: "I'll be over about eight o'clock tonight."

Will: "Okay. If I'm studying, wake me up."

Age

Asking a woman her age is like buying a secondhand car. The odometer has been set back, but you can't tell how far.

Strange

A foreigner commented: "You Americans are strange people. You devote one day out of the year to your mothers, and an entire week to pickles."

Too Late

Backward, turn backward, O Time, in thy flight—I've just thought of a wisecrack I needed last night.

That Explains It

In a small restaurant in Texas, a traveler ordered two fried eggs and was surprised that he was charged a dollar apiece for them. He asked the proprietor, "Are eggs scarce around here?"

"No," replied the owner, "but tourists are."

Wasn't Impressed

A penniless writer was approached by his landlord who demanded that he pay up his back due rent.

"You don't know what you're doing to yourself," the writer said. "Twenty years from now people will come by and look at this house and say, 'Clark, the famous novelist once lived here.'"

The landlord was unimpressed. "Clark, I'm telling you that if you don't pay your rent, they'll be saying that day after tomorrow."

Near-Sighted

A workman had climbed a steep ladder and was perched precariously on the rim of the city hall clock. He was cleaning the huge dial when a passerby stopped to watch.

"What's wrong?" the passerby asked. "Is something wrong with the clock?"

"It's fine," replied the workman. "I'm just near-sighted."

At Least

A farmer and his wife were visiting a large city and stopped at a plush restaurant for lunch. The farmer studied the menu for awhile and then ordered hamburgers at $1.85 each. Then turning to his wife he casually remarked, "The way these people have figured it, we have a steer at home worth $50,000!"

Takes a Long Time

There is the story about the little boy in Moscow who answers the door and finds a stranger inquiring after the boy's father.

"He's not here," the boy says. "He's in outer space and won't be home until 11:32 a.m. tomorrow."

"And your mother?" asks the stranger.

"No one knows when she'll be back," the kid says. "She's standing in line at the butcher shop."

Be Careful

The office boy was rather nervous the first day of his new job. Summoning up courage, he approached his employer and said:

"Please, sir, I think you're wanted on the phone."

The employer, busy with his problems, replied:

"You think? What's the good of thinking?"

"Well, sir," the office boy said, "the voice at the other end said, 'Hello, is that you, you idiot?' "

Wrong Answer

Roll Call, the Capitol Hill newspaper, reports this switch on an old gag. The teacher was classifying a new pupil. "Who gave us this beautiful school?" she asked.

"President Johnson," he replied.

"Who gave us our transcontinental roads?"

"President Johnson."

"Who makes the flowers grow and the rain to fall?"

"God," said the pupil.

At which point came a voice from the rear, "Throw that Republican out!"—*Walter Trohan, Chicago Tribune Press Service*

A New Computer

The latest invention if one cannot sleep is a bedside computer for counting sheep.

Signs of the Times

On the back of a trailer truck: "Not so close—give us a brake." On the windshield of a small foreign car: "For sale or adoption." In a pawnshop window: "Signs—all kinds." Over the door of an aquarium and bird pet shop: "Fish and cheeps." At a used car lot: "For Sale: Pre-Owned Automobiles." And in the window of an antique dealer: "We have a complete set of what you don't need."

Correct—They Are

Grandpa got on the big four-engine jet to take his first plane ride. When the motors roared, he gripped the arms of his seat in terror and closed his eyes. About ten minutes later he looked up and out of the window. He turned to the man beside him. "Just as I expected. The people down there look just like ants."

"They are ants," the man explained. "We're still sitting on the runway!"

Golf Socks

"I'll have to wear my golf socks today," the husband grumbled aloud to his wife as he rummaged through the drawer.

"What golf socks?" she asked.

"The ones with the eighteen holes in them."

He Knew What He Wanted

A little boy had been pawing over a stationer's stock of greeting cards for a long time when a clerk asked him, "Can I help you find what you're looking for, son? Birthday card? Get-well card? Anniversary congratulations to your mother or dad?"

"Not exactly," said the little boy, shaking his head. Then wistfully, "You got anything in the line of blank report cards?"

Played Safe

Said the explorer: "As the tiger charged at me, I leaped for an overhanging branch twenty feet above the ground."

"Did you make it?" interrupted the tense listener.

"Not on the way up," the explorer replied, "but I was lucky enough to grab one on the way back down."

Just Resting

A woman opened her refrigerator and, lo, there was a rabbit inside. "What are you doing here?" she asked.

"Isn't this a Westinghouse?" replied the rabbit.

The woman said, "Yes."

"Well, I'm westing."

Nobody Working

Some hoboes were holding a bull session under a new overpass as streams of cars rolled overhead. "Holidays make me feel awful ordinary," said one. "All those people going on picnics and campouts. Ain't nobody working?"

To the Head of the Class

"Now, James," said the English teacher, "give me a sentence using the word 'archaic.' "

"We can't have archaic and eat it too."

It Wouldn't Be Easy

"Say, Jane, what's the greatest feat of strength on the map?" asked Jim.

"Wheeling, West Virginia, on the Ohio River," Jane answered promptly.

Plenty of Friends

The warden of the penitentiary began to feel sorry for one of the prisoners. On visitor's day, while most of the prisoners received kinfolk, this fellow sat alone in his cell.

One visiting day, the warden called him into his office. "Ben," he said kindly, "I notice you never have any callers. Don't you have any friends or family?"

"Oh, sure," replied Ben happily, "but they're all in here."

Mother Trouble

The school bus pulled up in front of the gate. Six-year-old Bobby appeared as his mother hustled him out of the door. Then the morning ritual began. Bobby dropped his books, laboriously picked them up, patted the dog, and struggled with the gate. His mother all but wrung her hands as she implored, begged, and threatened Bobby on his way. At last Bobby clambered on the bus.

"Are you having troubles this morning?" asked the bus driver.

"No," Bobby replied, "but I think my mother is."

Otherwise OK

Feeling ill one night a man went into the bathroom for an aspirin. In the dark he picked up a familiar-feeling bottle and helped himself to two pills. The next morning his wife came to breakfast excitedly and said: "Did you take some pills last night?"

"Yes," said the husband.

"Well," said the wife unhappily, "those pills were for my sweetpeas."

Choking sporadically, the man dashed to his doctor. After hearing his story and making a brief examination, the doctor said: "There's nothing to worry about: You've merely taken the equivalent of five bushels of sheep fertilizer!"

Yes They Do

"I don't plan to get married until I find a girl just like the girl who married my grandfather," the bachelor said.

"They don't make women like that any more," complained his friend who was also a bachelor.

"Oh, I don't know," said the first one. "Grandpa married this one just last week!"

We've Bought Some Too

A customer in the restaurant had complained about the pastry.

"I was making pastry before you were born," replied the indignant cook.

"Maybe," replied the customer, "but why sell it now?"

It Really Works

One farmer was telling another about a marvelous new scarecrow he devised. It was made of tin and not only waved its arms but also emitted a blood-curdling yell every few minutes.

His neighbor asked, "But does it really scare the crows?"

"Scare the crows!" exclaimed the farmer. "It scares them so bad they bring back the corn they stole last year!"

No Need to Worry

On an overseas flight, a jetliner ran into rough weather. After a while, the pilot made this announcement over the intercom:

"Ladies and gentlemen, I have an announcement to make. First of all, we're almost out of fuel, and the high winds have blown us off course. Second, we're making very good time."

Out All Night

A father had been lecturing his young hopeful on the evils of staying out late at night and getting up late in the morning.

"Remember that the early bird catches the worm, my boy."

"How about the worm, Father?" inquired the young man. "Wasn't he rather foolish to get up so early?"

"My son," replied the father solemnly, "that worm hadn't been to bed; he was on his way home."

Cheaper Rate

A man with a broken leg encased in a bulky cast wanted to visit relatives in another state. The earnest young airline representative sympathized with his problem, explaining that he would have to go first class and would probably require two seats.

"However," added the helpful young lady, "if you go in the middle of the week, your leg can travel family plan."

Smart Teller

The holdup man shoved a note at the bank teller ordering, "Hand me all the dough in your cage. I've got you covered."

The teller scribbled his reply, "Kindly go to the next window; I'm on my lunch hour."

Underpaid

An investigator was recently asked to check on reports that a farmer was paying his help below-standard wages. He went out to the farm and was introduced to the hired hands.

"This is Gordon," said the farmer. "He milks the cows and works in the fields and he gets $70 a week.

"This is Billy Joe, the other hired man. He works in the fields and tends the stock and gets $60 a week.

"And this young lady is Sue Ann. She cooks and keeps house and she gets $60 a week, room, and board.

"Fair enough so far," said the inspector. "Is there anyone else?"

"Only the half-wit," answered the farmer. "He gets $10 a week, room, and board."

"Aha," said the inspector. "I'd like to speak to him."

"You're talkin' to him right now," replied the farmer.

Don't Forget Next Time

They fed the computer at the Pentagon a series of questions, and the answer came out "yes."

The Admiral in charge asked the computer, "Yes—what?"

Back came the machine: "Yes, sir!"

Much Easier

During a baseball game in Los Angeles, a fan gave the visiting second baseman a terrible tongue-lashing. The fan's glee reached a climax in the 8th inning when the second baseman lost an easy pop fly in the glare of the lights and let an opposing runner score the tying run. When the inning ended, the unhappy second sacker trotted to the dugout muttering to himself. The jubilant fan said, "Why, you bum! I could have caught that one myself."

"Sure, you could," yelled back the player. "I only had my glove. You've got your mouth!"

SURE

A woman was discussing the English language with Rudyard Kipling.

"Don't you think it strange, Mr. Kipling," said the woman, with superior wisdom, "that sugar is the only word in the English language where an 's' and a 'u' come together and are pronounced 'sh'?"

Mr. Kipling's eyes twinkled as he answered: "Sure."

Then They All Go Up

One small boy to another as they were coming down an escalator: "I wonder what happens when the basement is full of steps?"

Expecting Too Much

"Yes," said the personnel manager to the job applicant, "what we're after is a man of vision; a man with drive, determination, fire; a man who can inspire others; a man who can pull our bowling team out of last place!"

This Will Drive Him Nutty

"And what is he doing now?"

"He's a mechanic in a candy factory."

"A mechanic in a candy factory?'"

"Yes, he tightens the nuts in the peanut brittle."

Economy

A man stopped at a motel and asked for a room.

"Do you want a $12 room or a $15 room?" asked the manager.

"What's the difference?"

"The $15 room has a free TV."

Is This Clear?

The luggage-laden husband stared miserably down the station platform at the departing train.

"If you hadn't taken so long getting ready," he complained to his wife, "we would have caught that train."

"Yes," she replied, "and if you hadn't hurried me so, we wouldn't have so long to wait for the next one!"

Not Exactly

The salesman took his young son to the zoo. They walked from cage to cage until they finally came to one containing a restive leopard.

"Daddy," asked little Johnny, "is that the dotted lion you're always talking about?"

He Means Business

The customer returned his monthly payment card to the bank's charge plan with his check. The card was not stapled, not folded, and not creased in any way, but did contain a correction in the spelling of his name and this neatly penned message: "Dear Machine: You have spelled my name wrong again. Please correct and acknowledge. If not corrected by next month, I shall bend your card."

Golf

Golf in North Carolina is a tradition—a way of life. A North Carolinian, when asked if he had played much golf lately, replied, "No, not much—only in the afternoons."

Wise Willie

A local store was selling out boys' clothing very low and Willie and his mother went to see the bargain show. They halted at the counter where boys' trousers were piled high, and mother said, "Now, Willie, pick the pair that takes your eye." The foxy lad surveyed with care the piles of trousers neat, and chose from those which bore the sign: "These pants cannot be beat."—*Evans Echoes*

Women Shoppers

They come in different sizes, some are small and some are large.

No matter what their prize is, their battle cry is—charge!
—*Evans Echoes*

Same Guy

Guide: "This is the Leaning Tower of Pisa."

Tourist: "Pisa—Pisa—let me think. No, that doesn't sound like the name of the contractor who built my garage, but it sure looks like his work."

That Was Nothing

The city man visiting a ranch for the first time decided he'd like to ride, but soon found himself sprawling in the dust.

"Boy, how that horse can buck!" he exclaimed.

"Buck!" snorted the cowboy. "She only coughed."

Cut Down the Loss

Ephraim, storekeeper in a small Virginia town, was greeted by a neighbor who consoled him on the loss of some of his merchandise during a fire.

"Did you lose much?" asked the friend.

"Not too much," came the laconic reply. "I'd just marked most of my stock down twenty percent."

Dutch Treat?

"You're sweet enough to eat," he said in accents warm and low.

"I do eat," said the sweet young thing. "Where shall we go?"

Little Funny

The Rev. Robert Stewart of Westminster Church, Decatur, Illinois, had this story in the Westminster Chimes newsletter.

"The other day while at the hospital talking to Chaplain Rice about the loss of two of my hats in church during the past two weeks . . . I was feeling rather badly about my loss . . . when the good chaplain said he remembered the same thing happening to him in church one time . . . but worse yet, in his case, they had just finished singing 'God Will Take Care of You.' "—*Presbyterian Progress*

Faithful to the End

A lovely young model was looking very glum. "What's the matter, Joan?" asked the photographer.

"It's my boyfriend," Joan explained. "He's lost all his money."

"Ah," the photographer was sympathetic, "and I'll bet you're sorry for him."

"Yes," said the model wistfully. "He'll miss me."

Everyone Is Happy

Chaos changed to quiet when the next-door neighbors, a family of nine, went on their vacation. A few days after they left, the stay-at-home neighbors received a colorful picture postcard saying, "How are you enjoying our vacation?"

Nothing Right

O'Halloran had just returned from a visit to the big city, ready to impress the villagers with his sophistication.

"The food at those big hotels was poison, poison!" he declared. "And to make matters worse, the portions were so small!"

Better Deal

Three-year-old Dick did not like soap and water. One day his mother was trying to reason with him. "Surely you want to be a clean little boy, don't you?"

"Yes," tearfully agreed Dick, "but can't you just dust me?"

Well, Maybe

Salesman: "Are you sure your boss isn't in his office?"
Receptionist: "Are you doubting his word?"

What's New Today?

At first I had a blonde love, and now a sleek brunette; tomorrow'll bring a redhead—I'll date all colors yet. You may think that I'm fickle, or that I can't be true; but these are all the same girl—it's just her hair that's new.

He Had Trouble Enough

When his ball dented a car in the club's parking lot, a conscientious golfer in California wrote a note on his business card and stuck it in the windshield: "I'm sorry my ball hit the top of your hood. Send me the bill."

A few days later he received a reply: "Thanks for your consideration. The damage is so minor I'm not going to bother. May I suggest that you spend the money this would have cost you to take a couple of golf lessons. Any man with a hook that bad needs no trouble from me; he's got plenty of his own."
—*Evans Echoes*

Smart Lad

A little boy was balancing himself on his head. An old lady who knew him came by.

"Aren't you too young to do that? You are only six," she said.

"It's all right, missis," replied the boy. "You see, I'm nine when I'm upside down."

Hard Question

"Daddy!" cried the boy.

"One more question, then," sighed the tired father.

"How far is it," inquired the tot, "between to and fro?"

How to Be a Leader

A politician was being interviewed by the press. One reporter asked, "Do you feel that you have influenced public opinion, sir?"

"No," he answered. "Public opinion is something like a mule I once owned. In order to keep up the appearance of being the driver, I had to watch the way he was going and follow closely."

Just Like Trading Stamps

"What am I to do with this?" grumbled the motorist as the police clerk handed him a receipt for his traffic fine payment.

"Keep it," the clerk advised. "When you get four of them, you get a bicycle."

It Won't Be Easy

Shoe department manager to customer: "Yes, we have quite a selection of loafers. I'll see if I can get one to wait on you."

Great Speech

Admirer to political candidate: "Great speech, sir. I liked the straightforward way you dodged those issues!"

It Was His Fault

Billy: "Mother, Bobby broke a window."

Mother: "How did he do it?"

Billy: "I threw a rock at him and he ducked."

It Wasn't Easy

The salesman was summoned to the business comptroller's office, told that his expense account was the subject of some amazement and was asked, "How do you manage to spend $18 a day for food?"

"I manage," he replied, "by skipping breakfast."

Long Wait

An elderly man was the last patient in a doctor's crowded waiting room. As the doctor examined him, he apologized for keeping the man waiting so long.

"Oh, I don't mind the wait so much," said the man, "but I thought you would prefer to treat my ailment in its early stages!"

She Enjoyed It

After having run into a wild crowd at the football game, the referee told his wife that evening that it might be better if she stayed away from the remaining games to which he was assigned.

"After all," he said, "it must have been pretty embarrassing to you when everyone around you stood up and booed me."

"It wasn't so bad," she replied. "I stood up and booed too."

Good Training for the Job

Two co-workers were discussing the fact that they both had youngsters who were away at college. "What does your boy plan to be when he graduates?" asked one man.

"I'm not really sure, but judging from the letters he writes home, I'd say he was going to be a professional fund raiser."

Hard Question

The teacher in a little country school was at the blackboard explaining arithmetic problems, and was delighted to see that the tall, gangling lad, her dullest pupil, was watching intently.

Her happy thought was that, at last, he was beginning to understand. So when she had finished, she said to him: "You were so interested, Cicero, that I'm certain you want to ask more questions."

"Yas'm," drawled Cicero, "I got one to ask—where do them numbers go when you rub 'em off the board?"

Modern Youth

A mother summed up the problems of parenthood by explaining, "My oldest is in college, and my youngest is in nursery school, and some days you can hardly tell the difference."

Deductions of a City Slicker

I would flee from the city's rule and law, from its fashion and form cut loose, and go where the strawberry grows on its straw, and the gooseberry on its goose; where the catnip tree is climbed by the cat as she crouches for her prey—the guileless and unsuspecting rat on the rattan bush at play.

I will watch at ease for the saffron cow and the cowlet in their glee, as they leap in joy from bough to bough on the top of the cowslip tree; where the musical partridge drums on his drum, and the woodchuck chucks his wood, and the dog devours the dogwood plum, in the primitive solitude.

And then to the whitewashed dairy I'll turn, where the dairymaid hastening hies, her ruddy and golden-haired butter to churn from the milk of her butterflies; and I'll rise at morn with the early bird, to the fragrant farmyard pass, when the farmer turns his beautiful herd of grasshoppers out to grass.

Mosquitos

They buzz around our heads at night, and pausing briefly in their flight, they light upon a knee or nose, or any part that we expose. For they are smarter than a fly, and faster than the mortal eye; and when we swat at one, we hit the place that it just left, and bit.

And Also Show My Movies

You must have had a nice vacation, the woods and ocean sound just fine. But hurry up and end your travels—I want to tell about mine.

It Certainly Is

It's easy to say what another should do in the struggle for glory or pelf, but when the same problems are put up to you, ain't it hard to decide for yourself?

An Idea

One harassed mother found a new use for her child's play-pen. Every afternoon she sits in it where her youngsters can't get at her, and she reads peacefully.

Out of the Stillness

It was an opening appearance of the Philadelphia Symphony Orchestra, with Stokowski at his most majestic. The music was crashing and thunderous, when suddenly there fell an abrupt and complete silence, beginning a brief but absolute rest in the music. Out of the still night there came a high-pitched feminine voice, full of reproach and finality: "But I always fry mine in butter."

For Husbands Only

Irate taxi driver to fare: "There'll be no charge, lady; you did most of the driving."

She Learned Fast

The other day I heard my five-year-old boy screaming in the playroom, and when I ran in I found the baby pulling his hair.

"Never mind," I tried to comfort him, "your baby sister doesn't understand that it hurts you."

I hadn't been out of the room for a minute when more shrieks sent me running back. This time the baby was crying.

"What's the matter with the baby?" I asked the boy.

"Nothing much," he replied calmly. "Only now she knows."

Still Are

The teacher asked a class, discussing the North American Indian, if anyone could tell what the leaders of the tribes were called.

"Chiefs," said a little girl.

"Correct," said the teacher. "And what were the women called?"

A sharp little lad answered promptly, "Mischiefs."

Bad Joke

A man was boasting of the fine qualities of his Volkswagen which had been among the first purchased in this country and telling what fine care he was taking of it.

A friend asked, "What are you going to do with it when it wears out, scrap it?"

"No," was the answer, "I am going to put it in an old Volks home."

Ditto

The Bank of England requires its employees to sign a daily register. If they are late for work, they have to record the reason on the register.

London weather being what it is, the first tardy worker generally writes "fog" opposite his name. And human nature being what it is, those who sign in after him just make ditto marks.

One morning, the first latecomer wrote in the book, "Wife had twins." Under this gentleman's name twenty people placed their ditto marks.

Pollution

"Just go out for a
breath of air . . .
And you'll be ready for
Medicare . . ."—*Tom Lehrer*

Doctor's Advice

A lady went to her doctor's office and found the door locked. On the doorknob hung a sign which read, "Gone on vacation. Back in two weeks. Cut down on everything."

Income Tax Report

A new simplified income tax form for next year:
1. What was your income last year?
2. What were your expenses?
3. How much have you left?
4. Send it in.

It Applies to Us

Willis: "I've taken three lessons in French from a correspondence school."

Gillis: "So. Could you carry on a conversation with a Frenchman?"

Willis: "Oh no, but I could talk to anybody else who had had three lessons."

Hollow

A larger-than-average man stepped on the scales, not knowing they were out of order. The indicator stopped at seventy-five pounds.

A little boy standing by watched him intently. "Whaddaya know," he marveled. "He's hollow!"

No Discount

"How much is a ticket to Cleveland?" asked the little old lady at the railway ticket window.

"Ten dollars and 79 cents," the agent said.

The woman turned to the little girl beside her. "I guess we may as well buy from him. I've asked at all these windows and they all charge the same price."

Foresight

One of the horde of Washington apartment dwellers reports a new twist in Christmas cards. He got one the other day. It was from the superintendent of his building. Inside the card was a small return envelope.—*Les Carpenter*

No Use Testing Him

A mother called to make arrangements to enter her son in school. The admission officer explained the usual requirements, and asked the parents' approval of giving the boy a number of aptitude tests. The mother said, "Everything is O.K. with me, but I don't see any sense in giving any apt-to-do tests because I can tell you right now that that boy's apt to do most anything. —*Arthur I. Cates*

Reasonable

A small girl, enchanted with her new baby cousin, asked her mother, "Can't we have a baby?"

"I don't believe so, darling," said her mother. "They cost too much."

"How much?" inquired the child.

"Oh, about $200," said the mother.

The youngster thought a moment. "That's not very much, when you consider how long one would last."

Could Be

When a woman whose parked car rolled into another car in a California community was asked by a policeman, "Why didn't you set your emergency brake?" She replied. "Emergency? Is mailing a letter an emergency?"

Hard Battle

"Jimmy, what's all that racket in the kitchen?" called Mother anxiously.

"I'm fighting temptation," answered Jimmy.

A Sure Sign

Spring is here with balmy breezes, sunshine smiles upon us all. Trees and grass regain their color, open spaces seem to call.

All foretell the approach of summer, but the surest sign is seen when the sand is in the tee-box and the flag is on the green.

Greek to Some of Us

A couple of Greek delegates to a conference in Britain were watching their first cricket match. After a while, one mystified Greek turned to the other and pleaded for enlightment.

Said the other throwing up his hands: "I don't know, either. It's all English to me!"

Doing Well

In any business group, one of the major questions is, how is business. You might be interested in the comment made by one of my associates the other day when he was asked, "How is business?"

He said, "Well, we are eleven meetings ahead of the same time last year."—*James Henry Binger*

Isn't That Clear?

A Frenchman was complaining to an American, saying, "Ze English language is very funny. When you Americans say 'fat chance' it means ze same as 'slim chance.'"

Right

It ain't braggin' if you done it.—*Dizzy Dean*

Fast Travel

With regard to how fast you travel, this reminds me that I was in the airport in Zurich the other day coming back with a fellow from Chicago. He had had a rhubarb with Swiss Air over his confirmation in Europe. You have to reconfirm your trip back.

He asked them as to how soon before you left Europe you were supposed to reconfirm. They told him he had to reconfirm seventy-two hours before he left Europe. He then replied, "Well at that point I still had not bought my ticket in Chicago." —*R. J. Rutherford*

The American Way

After years of study and untangling of much red tape, the refugee couple finally managed to gain their citizenship.

The husband rushed into the kitchen with the good news. "Anna, Anna!" he shouted. "At last we are American citizens."

"How wonderful, how wonderful!" Anna replied. "Now you can do the dishes."

That Helps

A wildly excited man ran into the police station shouting, "I need help! A man just stole my car!"

"Did you see him?" asked the desk officer.

"No, but I got the licence number as he pulled away."

He Is Really Meek

One housewife to another: "Has she trained her husband to be meek?"

"He's as apologetic as a near-sighted porcupine wandering in a cactus garden."

The Same Everywhere

The traffic experts asked the mayor how the new road-building program was affecting the city.

"Now we have congestion in places," explained the mayor, "where before we didn't even have places."

Common Practice

"You pay a small deposit," said the salesman, "and then make no more payments for six months."

"Who told you about us?" demanded the lady of the house.

Golf

In Africa, some native tribes practice the strange custom of beating the ground with clubs and uttering wild, blood-curdling yells. Anthropologists call this a form of primitive expression. In America, we call it golf.

That Much?

A minister, in closing his sermon, said: "And now, brethen, let us all give in accordance with what we reported in our income tax."

There Is a Difference

A bachelor philosopher was introduced by a matchmaker friend to a lady who was known for her brilliance. After a two-hour conversation in which the lady did all the talking, Spencer was asked by the friend:

"What did you think of her? She has a great mind, hasn't she?"

"No," replied Spencer, "she has a small mind, but it's certainly very active."

Too Close

"How close did it come to you?" asked the farmer, driving up to the tree where his hired man had taken shelter from an electrical storm one morning.

"Well," stammered the hired man, "I don't know, but my pipe wasn't lit before."

No Signatures

A principal, proud of a newly painted wall in his school, had the following sign put up: "This is a partition, not a petition. No signatures are required."

Naturally

Teacher (sternly): "This essay on 'Our Dog' is word for word the same as your brother's."

Small boy: "Yes, sir, it's the same dog."

Better Informed

New Pastor: What did you think of the sermon last Sunday?

Parishioner: Very good, indeed, sir. So instructive. We really didn't know what sin was till you came here.

Easy to Do

Housewife to butcher: Please send me a dollar's worth of steak. Tell the boy to push it through the keyhole, if I'm not home.

Say That Again

"Sedentary work," said the college lecturer, "tends to lessen the endurance."

"In other words," butted in the smart student, "the more one sits, the less one can stand."

"Exactly," retorted the lecturer; "and if one lies a great deal, one's standing is lost completely."

Modern Youth

"Now, son, there is a wonderful example in the life of an ant," pointed out the father. "Every day the ant goes to work and works all day. Every day the ant is busy. And, in the end what happens?"

Unimpressed, the boy replied, "Someone steps on him."

Good Idea

Small boy, just home from school: "I learned something new from the school psychologist today. It's called 'spanking.' "

Could Be

Little boy: "What does PTA mean? Mom talks about it."
Second little boy: "I think it means Poor Tired Adults."

Good Deal

There is a rumor going around that we now have a new trade agreement with Russia. We're sending them 3,000 cars from Detroit and they're sending us 20,000 parking spaces from Siberia.

Valuable Information

Only male crickets chirp, only male lightning bugs light up, and only female mosquitoes bite.

Tricksters

My wife can make money go far, and she does so with some insistence. In fact, she can make it go so far that it vanishes in the distance.

Don't Give Up Hope

He was one of those tourists who liked to brag about the number of miles covered in a day. As the evening wore on they passed motel after motel with the "No Vacancy" sign out.

Finally, the patient wife remarked, "I know we'll find one soon dear. People are starting to get up."

Appreciation

Humans are a simple breed, yet kindly in their way; they'll travel miles at breakneck speed on a hot and dusty day, and scramble through the biggest bunch of poison ivy plants to bring a lovely, tasty lunch to all us hungry ants.

Simple

A New Jersey newspaper polled over 1,000 students for their views on preventing classroom cheating. More than 21 percent of the students queried came up with a foolproof plan: To end cheating, stop giving exams.

Introducing the Speaker

The secretary of a ladies' luncheon club rose to present the speaker of the day. "Normally," she said with her brightest smile, "this honor would fall to our president, who has never missed hearing any of our speakers. But today she is in Atlantic City—and how we all envy her!"

Arithmetic

Women have a passion for arithmetic. They divide their ages by two, double the price of their dresses, treble their husbands' salaries, and add five years to the ages of their best friends.

The Easy Way

"Why does it take three of you guys to change a burnt-out light bulb?" asked the foreman.

"Well," retorted the assistant, "Jim holds the bulb while Frank and I turn the ladder."

Not Too Difficult

Fire Chief: "Since we have only one fire engine, what would you do if you were left in charge while we were away and another fire was reported?"

Recruit: "Tell the caller to keep it going until you got back."

All OK

My husband thoughtfully bought me an electric blanket, since I always complain about cold sheets. I was a little reluctant to sleep under all that electric wiring, but he assured me it was safe, and in no time I was dozing off contentedly.

What my husband did not know was that I had put a ham in the oven to bake all night at low heat. When he awoke in the night and smelled something cooking, he reached over and shook me. "Darling!" he cried. "Are you all right!"

CHAPTER 5

BIOGRAPHICAL ILLUSTRATIONS

Progress

I believe every address, like every sermon, should start with a text, and given the title of my speech today, "The British Economy After Devaluation," I can't think of a better one than one of Samuel Butler's truisms in which he said, "All progress is based upon a universal desire on the part of every organism to live beyond its income."—*Sir Patrick Dean, British Ambassador to the United States*

Pronunciation

To remind ourselves of the long tradition of cooperation between our countries is not to ignore our differences. I am reminded of Hershfield's account of a certain campaign joined by British and American forces towards the end of the last war. When General Montgomery asked whether American troops could take a certain sector of the line, General Eisenhower promised that it would be taken "on schedule." "Where," General Montgomery demanded, in his crisp British accent, "did you learn to pronounce the word shed-shuel?" Replied General Eisenhower: "In grammar shuul."—*Sir Patrick Dean, British Ambassador to the United States*

George Bernard Shaw

When George Bernard Shaw was seventy, he was asked how he felt and he replied, "at my age you either feel great or not at all."

Don't Speak English

Senate Democratic Leader Mike Mansfield reports two Brooklyn truck drivers were hauling a cargo across country and into Canada. It was their first visit to our northern neighbor.

Late in the evening they stopped in a large town, parked their truck and entered a diner, where a waitress set glasses of water and cutlery in front of them.

"What town is this?" the first driver asked.

"Saskatoon, Saskatchewan."

"Boy, are we in a mess," said the second driver. "They don't even speak English here."

He Misses Sometimes

Rep. Wilbur Mills (D., Ark.), chairman of the House Ways and Means Committee, says that in receiving various federal budgets he frequently finds himself in the position of a producer who was interviewing acts for a stage show.

"My beautiful partner and I do acrobatics," said one applicant for a part in the production, "and, as a thrilling climax, I whirl her around my head twenty times and fling her through a closed window."

"Great scott," exclaimed the producer. "Do you do that in every act?"

"No, sometimes I miss the window."

Fifty-Fifty

Charles M. Schwab used to tell of a southern railway man who came into the office of the Carnegie Company in Pittsburgh years ago to negotiate for steel for his new road. The price of the rails was entirely satisfactory, the quality taken for granted, and all was well so far. Mr. Schwab knew from long experience, however, what was coming next.

"Now in payment, Mr. Schwab, will you take bonds of the new railroad?"

"Oh, yes," assented Mr. Schwab.

"You will?" asked the astonished promoter. "On what basis?"

"Fifty-fifty," answered Mr. Schwab, "a ton of bonds for a ton of rails."

Right Idea

Some years ago former Congressman Brooks Hayes from Arkansas was always pretty sure of reelection, so he had time to campaign for deserving Democrats in other states. He always had a few good stories.

One he used to get by with tremendously was the story about his little Baptist Church in his home town in Arkansas, where there was some agitation to buy a chandelier. They had a meeting of the board of deacons to discuss it; and the first two deacons that spoke, spoke in favor of it.

The third deacon stood up and said, "I'm agin it, this proposal, and I'm agin it for three reasons. In the first place there ain't nobody here knows how to spell the word, so we couldn't order one.

"In the second place, even if we happened to get one there is nobody in the congregation that knows how to play it. And in the third place, if the church has any extra money to spend I think they ought to buy a new lighting fixture."—*Elmer Roper*

Discovering a New World

Although legend tells us that Queen Isabella pawned her jewels in order to finance the voyages of Christopher Columbus, recent investigations prove this to be pure fiction. She said she would be willing to do it, but as Columbus raised the needed funds, it never became necessary. It has been figured out that the cost of the expedition amounted to seven thousand, two hundred and fifty dollars. Of this sum, Columbus received for himself three hundred and twenty dollars. The captains of the other two ships got one hundred and eighty dollars each, and the sailors about twenty-nine dollars each. The equipment of the vessels cost two thousand, eight hundred and twenty-five dollars.—*Sunshine Magazine*

Planning Ahead

When they honored Lefty O'Doul, the great baseball player, at his party on his 70th birthday in San Francisco, the old slugger said: "I'm finally learning to save my money. When I get to be 80, I'm going to throw the damndest birthday bash you ever saw."

Quotations From Will Rogers

I never met a man I didn't like.

In the early days of the Indian Territory, there were no such things as birth certificates. Your being there was certificate enough.

I had just enough white in me to make my honesty questionable.

Being a hero is about the shortest-lived profession on earth.

I don't make jokes—I just watch the government and report the facts.

The United States never lost a war or won a conference.

(Of his first book, "The Cowboy Philosopher on the Peace Conference") I made this book short so you could finish it before the next war.

(Of the Income Tax) It has made more liars out of the American people than golf.

(Of President Coolidge) He is the first President to discover that what the American people want is to be left alone.

(On being made Mayor of Beverly Hills) I have never seen a Mayor that wasn't funny and the minute he puts on a Silk Hat, he becomes Screamingly Funny . . . What the country needs is more ex-Mayors.

(Of missionaries) Any nation is heathen that ain't strong enough to punch you in the jaw . . . Missionaries teach 'em not only how to serve the Lord but run a Ford car . . . then the American Agent sells 'em one . . . You take religion backed up by Commerce and it's awful hard for a heathen to overcome.

(Of a Mississippi flood) One rowboat would do more for you in a flood than all the Senators in Washington talking about you . . . I got more faith in high ground than in any Senator I ever saw.

(Of the Stock Market) Just as Mr. Brisbane and I have been constantly telling you, Don't Gamble; take all your savings and buy some good stock, and hold it till it goes up, then sell it. If it don't go up, don't buy it.

It Was Simple

The following is said to have been turned in by a school boy who was told to write a composition on that momentous event which transpired in October, 1492:

"One day the king of Spain sent for Columbus and asked: 'Can you discover America?'

" 'Yes,' Columbus answered, 'if you will give me some boats and sailors.'

"He got the boats and sailed in the direction in which he knew America was. The sailors mutinied and swore there was no such place as America, but finally the pilot came to Columbus and said: 'Captain, land is in sight.'

"When the boat neared the shore, Columbus saw a bunch of natives. 'Hey! Hey!' he yelled to them. 'Is this America?'

" 'Yes,' they replied.

" 'Then I suppose you are Indians,' Columbus went on.

" 'Yes,' replied the chief, 'and you are Christopher Columbus, I take it?'

" 'I am,' said Columbus.

"The Indian chief then turned to his fellow savages and said, 'The jig is up, guys. We're discovered!' " — *Sunshine Magazine*

The concern for man and his destiny must always be the chief interest of all technical effort. Never forget it among your diagrams and equations.—*Albert Einstein's Philosophy*

Getting Fun Out of Life

Benjamin Franklin at 78 had fun being Ambassador to France.

Michelangelo at 79 although an artist, had fun writing sonnets.

Sophocles, at 90, had fun writing Oedipus Rex.

Titian, at 98 had fun painting his "Battle of Lepanto."

Oliver Wendell Holmes at 91, had fun writing his dissenting opinions as Associate Justice of the Supreme Court.

—*E. W. Ireland in Dynamic Maturity*

Greatness

If you want to be a bigger, better person, think big, mingle with big people, and act big. A few years ago a woman died in Paris who had the dubious reputation of being "the best dressed woman in Europe." After her decease, it was found that she had a wardrobe which contained almost a thousand frocks . . . A thousand frocks and only one life to live! . . . A few years earlier, there died in London a man who had only one suit of clothes. It was a blue suit with a red collar on the coat. That man was William Booth, the founder of the Salvation Army. He had only one suit but in the course of his life he lived a thousand lives. He acted big.—*S. Robert Weaver, Watchman-Examiner*

Youth

Mozart was 8 when he composed his first symphony.

Alexander the Great made his major military conquests while he was in his twenties.

Albert Einstein published his first articles on the theory of relativity when he was 26.

Jane Addams founded Hull House when she was 29.

Alexander Graham Bell patented the telephone when he was 29.

Michelangelo completed his famous "Pieta" by the age of 26.

Samuel Colt patented his first revolver in his early twenties.

John Keats wrote most of his best-known poems when he was 23.

Age

Cervantes completed Don Quixote when he was nearing 70.

Clara Barton, at 59, founded the American Red Cross.

Goethe finished the dramatic poem "Faust" at 82.

Verdi composed Otello at 73, Falstaff in his late seventies.

Leonardo da Vinci painted the "Mona Lisa" when he was about 50.

Dostoevski wrote his first great novel, "Crime and Punishment," at 45.

Benjamin Disraeli became Prime Minister of England for the second time at 70.

George Washington

Washington's is the mightiest name on earth—long since mightiest in the cause of civil liberty; still mightiest in moral reformation. On that name no eulogy is expected. It cannot be. To add brightness to the sun, or glory to the name of Washington, is alike impossible. Let none attempt it. In solemn awe we pronounce the name, and in its naked, deathless splendor leave it shining on.—*Abraham Lincoln*

Art

From early youth until his death at the age of 78, through periods of poverty and crippling arthritis, Auguste Renoir, the French painter, devoted himself fanatically to his work.

Shortly before he breathed his last, he looked up at those gathered at his bedside and murmured: "What a pity! I was just beginning to show a little promise."—*Milwaukee Journal*

Bad Either Way

While visiting her former hometown, Dagmar Godowsky reminisced about her father, Leopold Godowsky, the noted pianist who died in 1938. She recalled they once attended a concert at which the pianist played very badly. As he played Miss Godowsky whispered to her father, "Isn't it awful how much he forgets?"

To which her father replied sadly, "What he remembers is worse."

The Price

On one occasion a lady said to a famous violinist: "I would give half my life to be able to play like you do."

"That, madam," he replied, "is exactly what I have given to do it."

And it was Leonardo da Vinci, the great painter and philosopher, who exclaimed: "Thou, O God, dost sell us all good things at the price of labor."

Showmanship

Benjamin Franklin will be remembered by every school-child because of his dramatic "key and kite" experiment. Newton may not have first pondered gravity after being hit on the head by an apple, but it makes a good story.

There is also a story told about Galileo. In order to prove his theory of "falling bodies," it is said that he took a ten-pound and a half-pound ball atop the Tower of Pisa and let them fall simultaneously. There is nothing to substantiate this story of showmanship, but Galileo will long be associated with falling balls and the Leaning Tower of Pisa.

Galileo also was associated with vacuum studies. He tried for many years to achieve the perfect vacuum by filling a cylinder with water then removing a piston. He died before he was able to accomplish the desired results, but his pupil and friend Evangelista Torricelli did what Galileo could not. After sealing one end of a three-foot tube, he filled it with mercury, and stood the open end in a dish of mercury. The mercury in the tube fell until it was about thirty inches above the surface of the mercury in the bowl.

Torricelli not only produced the vacuum Galileo couldn't but also invented an instrument for recording atmospheric pressure, the barometer. Few remember Torricelli, yet showman Galileo will forever live in science books.—*Sunshine Magazine*

Self Expression

Winston Churchill, possibly the world's greatest talker, was unquestionably its worst listener. In the House of Commons, one time, while listening to a member of the opposition, he began to shake his head, and got more attention than the speaker, who, finally, unable to control himself, aimed a forefinger at Churchill, shouting, "I wish to remind the Right Honorable friend that I am only expressing my own opinion."

Impishly looking up, Churchill answered, "And I wish to remind the speaker that I am only shaking my own head."

Communists

Willy Brandt of West Germany, defining the Communists' view of coexistence: "They want to have their cake and eat ours too."

Famous Hoosiers

How many of you can remember the delightful stories of Gene Stratton Porter, who was really a scientist—"The Song of the Cardinal"; and "The Girl of the Limberlost"; "Freckles" and "Laddie."

Booth Tarkington wrote "Penrod"; "Seventeen"; "The Gentleman from Indiana," and a thousand others.

Meredith Nicholson, who wrote "The House of 1000 Candles"; "The Brown Jug of Kildare."

George Barr McCutcheon, who wrote "Graustark."

Edward Eggleston, who wrote "The Hoosier School Boy" —"Circuit Rider Roxy"—which were delightful tales of that day.

Charles Major, who wrote "When Knighthood Was in Flower" and "Dorothy Vernon of Haddon Hall"; "The Bears of Blue River," a delightful story for boys of any generation.

General Lew Wallace, who wrote "Ben Hur;" "The Prince of India."

Maurice Thompson, who wrote "Alice of Old Vincennes," "Witchery," and so many others.

David Graham Phillips; Don Herrold; John T. McCutcheon, whose "Injun' Summer" still appears annually on the front of the Tribune; and William Dudley Foulke, the founder of the Civil Service in the United States. And Julia Levering; Jeanette Nolan; Elmer Davis; Alvin Fay Harlow; and Theodore Dreiser, whose sister, Caroline, many years ago frightened Hoosiers out of their wits; and H. Allen Smith; Paul Dresser —their names are legend.

In poetry we haven't been very strong. We produced James Whitcomb Riley, but he was more painter than poet. He did write "The Raggedy Man," and "Little Orphant Annie," who comes to our house every day; and "There Little Girl Don't Cry"—"They Have Broken Your Dolly"—as delightful and sentimental a little poem as was every written.

The least known, however, appeared sometimes in the Tribune, and once every week on Saturday in the Indianapolis News, was James Buchanan Elmore, the Bard of Alamo.

Those of you who attended Wabash College will recall he came every Spring to recite his poetry on the campus of Crawfordsville. He wrote "The Wreck of the Monon." I could recite it but I believe I'll spare you. He also wrote an epitaph for the tombstone of his departed sweetheart, which we think is the formation of the triple negative. The poem went after this style:

> "She may be gone,
> But she's never forgotten;
> Never will, no, never not."

I will say you have to love them to speak about them that way.

Then he wrote the one on "O Sassafras":

> "O Sassafras, thou art the Sassafras
>   for me;
> And in the Spring, I love to sing,
> O Sassafras for me."

But the most important man we have in writing is Abe Martin, and you can still read Abe Martin in Chicago. He said, "You must remember it is no disgrace to be poor, but it might as well be." He also said, "The first thing to turn green in the Spring is Christmas jewelry." But this one rings true to some of us: "The best thing about automobiles is that relatives can go home the same day."

And about that delightful little sweetheart from Nashville, Fran Lippincott, who he said was confined to her home for the weekend by a swollen dresser drawer.

He also said, "Whenever you hear a man say, 'It's not the money; it's the principle,' you can bet it's the money."

They concentrated in music with Cole Porter and Hoagy Carmichael, with new trends in rhythm; in Wall Street, with K. C. Hogate and Bernard Kilgore, who tried new ideas in informing investors through the Wall Street Journal and Dow Jones; in Alcatraz with John Dillinger and Eugene V. Debs; and if you don't think we have variety, brother, you are mistaken!

But all of these pale into insignificance when we arrive in the political arena. We had one President, and we have had four Vice Presidents—Colfax, Hendricks, Fairbanks, and Marshall, whom some of you may have remembered.

Senators—we had Daniel W. Voorhees, the tall sycamore of the Wabash; Samuel Ralston; Preston Vannuys, and William Ezra Jenner, who spoke once here. He's the last of our "fairgrounds orators," and a delightful Republican. He never did change. The public did, but his chart looks like a yo-yo. Then Senator Watson and Paul Voorhees McNutt; the remarkable Wendell Willkie; Homer Capehart; and even Mrs. Barry Goldwater.

Of these great politicians we had one who went to jail; one who pleaded the Statute of Limitations; one who was impeached; and one of them said he was president of the best Senate that money could buy.

But there are only two that I think that really are the champs. They are both deceased so I may speak freely of them.

One was Senator James Eli Watson, the Master of Humbug, and a delightful man. He was 35 years representing Indiana in the Halls of Congress, and he had a delightful sense of humor.

He made one of the most pontifical statements about politics ever written: he said, "Don't worry about a political platform. It's like a railroad platform. It's not to stand on; it's to get in on."

One of his enemies died over at Rushville, one time, and he was asked, "Are you going to his funeral?"

He said, "No, but I approve of it."

Then he used the overhand stroke in making, or trying to solicit votes, and he was a master. He would always go back to Rushville, and Judge Sparkles, on the Circuit Court of Appeals, told me this story one time. He was the Judge of Rushville, and one of the very few who ever moved to the Circuit Court of Appeals from a circuit job, but he said, "Jim would come back to Rushville; and one time he was going around the courthouse square, using the overhand stroke and he came to a young man and he asked, "how is your father?"

The boy said, "Senator, he's dead."

He said, "I'm very sorry." He didn't have the foggiest notion of who the man was, but he said:

"We have always regarded him as a stalwart member of the community, and I hope you tell your mother that I am much bereaved at his passing."

He continued on around the circle, and he saw a young boy, and went to him and using his overhand stroke he asked, "Boy, how is your father?"

The boy said, "Senator, he's still dead."

The one who counterbalances him, rather, on the Democratic side, was Thomas Riley Marshall, who was one of the most delightful characters in all Hoosierdom.

He was the one who said—of course you remember it best, "What this country needs is a good five-cent cigar."

He told me a story one time, which I think is much better.

When he was presiding one man arose and said, "I'm like the great commoner, Henry Clay—I'd rather be right than be President."

And he said, "You don't need to worry, Mr. Flanagan, you're never going to be either one."

You know, he also would partake of wine once in a while, and all of his life he claimed that he and his beloved wife never spent one night away from each other. He one time said in her presence, "You know, in my lifetime I have made 10,000 speeches."

She said, "No, Honey, you've made the same speech 10,000 times."

Thomas Marshall also wrote his autobiography, and it's thoroughly delightful from beginning to end. He wrote this statement about his parents: He said, "I have known many people with finer education; of broader vision, and more potent influence in the affairs of men; but if love of humanity; dedication to virtue; and veneration of God be the mark of the perfect man and the perfect woman, I do not hesitate to lay the wreath upon the tomb of my father and my mother."

You have to be pretty good to say that.

Well, those are the Hoosiers; and at one time one of our governors said, "You can go further and do worse, and you probably will."

But at any rate, I think the record is pretty good.

Thank you.—*Roger D. Branigin, then Governor of Indiana*

George Washington

When George Washington took the oath as first President of the United States on April 30, 1789, he spontaneously added this four-word prayer of his own: "So help me God," an invocation still used in official oaths by those taking public office, in courts of justice, and in other legal proceedings.

I Am an American!

Patrick Henry has come down to posterity on the strength of a single quote—"Give me liberty or give me death!" This is manifestly unfair. The great Virginian said many notable—and quotable—things. For example, at the first Continental Congress it was he who struck the keynote: "The distinctions between Virginians, Pennsylvanians, New Yorkers, and New Englanders are gone. I am not a Virginian, but an American."

Two Great Teachers

I pay tribute to two of the world's illustrious. These two were teachers. We associate great teaching with the name of the one. For many years we have said, "Mark Hopkins on one end of a log and a student on the other constitute a university." We understand this high tribute to Mark Hopkins when we hear his words, "The outcome of a college training ought to be a sound body, a disciplined mind, a liberal education, a right character.

"He who carries the torchlight into the recesses of science, and shows the gems that are sparkling there, must not be a mere hired conductor, who is to bow in one company, and bow out another, and show what is to be seen with a heartless indifference, but must have an ever living fountain of emotion that will flow afresh as he contemplates anew the words of God and the great principles of truth and duty."

The other, Louis Braille, blinded early in his youth, invented the dot system we call the Braille method of reading. He developed the system that the blind "might evolve personalities as natural and resourceful as those of the seeing." The candle he lighted has been a light unto the pathway of countless thousands.

No Busy Signal Then

The first telephone in the White House was installed December 1, 1878, when Rutherford B. Hayes was in office. It was placed in a booth just outside the executive office. Since the President didn't use the phone very often, an aide answered the few calls that came in and usually spoke for him. Conditions remained the same until, in 1929, Herbert Hoover ordered a phone installed on his desk.

Faith

One of the great American authors, Nathaniel Hawthorne, not only owed his success to the inspiration of his wife, but also his only opportunity to compose his literary masterpiece.

If it had not been for Sophia, perhaps we should not now remember Nathaniel. He lost his job in the customhouse. A brokenhearted man, he went home to tell his wife that he was a failure. To his amazement she beamed with joy. "Now," she said, "you can write your book!"

To his bitter rejoinder, "Yes, and what shall we live on while I am writing it?" the astounding woman opened a drawer and took out an unsuspected hoard of cash. "Where on earth did you get that?" he cried.

She answered, "'I have always known you were a man of genius. I knew that someday you would write an immortal masterpiece. So every week, out of the money you have given me for housekeeping, I have saved something. Here is enough to last us one whole year."

Hawthorne sat down that very day and began writing the best story of his career—"The Scarlet Letter."

He Liked Rubber

If Charles Goodyear, the discoverer of the process of vulcanization, could have had his way, it would be a snap to stretch a dollar, even in these days of ultra-inflation. Goodyear was so enthusiastic about rubber that he wanted to have everything made out of rubber, and even tried to persuade the government to print its money on rubber. Many of the books in his library were specially bound in rubber, and he even had his autobiography printed and bound in rubber.—*Sunshine Magazine*

Criticism

It is a matter of record that George Washington had a difficult second term. When I consider the weak, inconsequential things the papers say about me, compared to what they said about him, who I think is the greatest human the English-speaking race has produced, then I can be philosophical.
—*Dwight D. Eisenhower*

Randolph and Clay

John Randolph and Henry Clay, once had a quarrel in the Senate at Washington. For several weeks they did not speak. When one day they met on Pennsylvania Avenue, each saw the other coming up the sidewalk which was very narrow at that point, and each was meditating as to how far he would turn out for the other to pass. As Randolph came up he looked the grand old Kentuckian straight in the eye and, keeping the sidewalk, hissed:

"I never turn out for scoundrels!"

"I always do," said Mr. Clay as he stepped politely out into the mud and let Randolph have the walk.

President Only for a Day!

Previous to 1934, the 4th of March was the day on which the Presidents of the United States were inaugurated into office.

In 1849, March 4 fell on a Sunday. President-elect Zachary Taylor, an outspoken individualist, declined to be sworn in on that day, saying, "It's the Lord's Day. Let us wait until Monday." And it did. For that one day, Sunday, Taylor named a friend, U. S. Senator from Missouri David Rice Atchison, to represent him, unofficially of course.

When Senator Atchison died in 1886, the state of Missouri appropriated $15,000 for his monument, which bears this inscription:

"David Rice Atchison, 1807-1886, President of the United States for one day. Lawyer, Statesman, and Jurist."

CHAPTER 6

HELPFUL MATERIAL FOR SPECIAL DAYS

Special events, "days," and "weeks" are observed throughout our country. Some of them might cause you to smile and wonder "what next?"

Here are a few that you may not have heard about: Break-a-Cold Month; Silent Record Week; Pencil Week; Buzzard Day; National Artichoke Week; National Insect Electrocutor Week; Fresh-Up Soda Bath Season; Back-to-Work Week; National Save-the-Horse Week; National Indigestion Month.

No matter how "far out" Americans go in celebrating special events, there are two holidays that stand out far and above all the others in the minds of young and old. Thanksgiving and Christmas are an integral part of life in America, and though many phases of life have changed in recent years, still the basic celebrations of these two seasons are based on the good old-fashioned spirit of friendship and goodwill.

A. NEW YEAR

The first thing that's broken after Christmas is a New Year's resolution.

* * *

He that resolves to mend hereafter resolves not to mend now!

* * *

No one ever regarded the first of January with indifference.
—*Charles Lamb*

The festivities of New Year's Day are of very ancient origin. In England the head of the house assembled his family around a bowl of spiced ale, from which he drank their healths; he then passed the bowl to others that they might also drink. The expression exchanged was Wass hael (To your health)—hence, the "wassail bowl" in subsequent celebrations. The poorer class of people carried the bowl adorned with ribbons through the neighborhood, begging for contributions. In their compotations they sang songs suitable to the occasion. This custom was also observed in monasteries and private homes. In front of the abbot, at the head of the refectory table, was placed such a bowl, called Coculum Caritatis (Bowl of Charity).

* * *

A little less impatient with those we deem too slow;
A little less of arrogance because of all we know;
A little more humility, seeing our worth is slight;
We are such trivial candles compared to stars at night!
A little more forgiving and swifter to be kind;
A little more desirous the word of praise to find;
The word of praise to utter and make a heart rejoice;
A little bit more careful to speak with gentle voice;
A little more true eagerness to understand each other;
A little more real striving to help a shipwrecked brother;
A little more high courage to each task that must be done;
These be our resolutions—and God help everyone!

—*Anonymous from Worden & Risberg bulletin*

* * *

Alas! how swift the moments fly!
How flash the years along!
Scarce here, yet gone already by,
The burden of a song.
See childhood, youth, and manhood pass,
And age with furrowed brow;
Time was—Time shall be—drain the glass—
But where in Time is now?

—*John Quincy Adams, The Hour Glass*

Time has laid his hand
Upon my heart, gently, not smiting it,
But as a harper lays his open palm
Upon his harp, to deaden its vibrations.
—*Henry Wadsworth Longfellow, "The Golden Legend"*

* * *

What is time? The shadow on the dial, the striking of the clock, the running of the sand, day and night, summer and winter, months, years, centuries—these are but arbitrary and outward signs, the measure of Time, not Time itself. Time is the Life of the soul.
—*Henry Wadsworth Longfellow, "Hyperion"*

* * *

Whether or not we admit it to ourselves, we are all haunted by a truly awful sense of impermanence. I have always had a particularly keen sense of this at New York cocktail parties, and perhaps this is why I drink the martinis almost as fast as I can snatch them from the tray.
—*Tennessee Williams, "The Timeless World of a Play"*

* * *

Many events, some important and others not so significant, have occurred on New Year's Day. Here are a few:

In the year 1000 many Christians expected the end of the world and gave away their belongings.

1673 saw the beginning of mail service between Boston and New York City.

1781 marked the revolt of the Pennsylvania Revolutionary troops because of lack of pay and horrible living conditions. They marched on Congress which was convened in Philadelphia at the time, but that august body fled before the angry soldiers reached the city.

In 1801, importation of slaves into this country was prohibited.

In 1863, Lincoln signed the Emancipation Proclamation.

A New Year's resolution is something that goes in one year and out the other.

B. VALENTINE DAY

St. Valentine, who lent his name to the holiday observed each year on February 14, actually had little to do with it. From a combination of pagan and Christian festivals has come this custom dedicated to love. In the late 1700s, sweethearts began penning and decorating cards, some so elegant and beautiful they are virtually museum pieces today. And since neither mail service nor envelopes existed, these tokens of love were usually delivered in person. The more well-to-do sent their cards by coach, though they double wrapped and sealed them with wax, so only their beloved could read them.

C. EASTER

Let us place more emphasis on the Easter heart than the Easter hat.

* * *

The great Easter truth is not that we are to live newly after death—that is not the great thing—but that we are to be new here and now by the power of the resurrection; not so much that we are to live forever as that we are to, and may, live nobly now because we are to live forever.—*Phillips Brooks*

* * *

Tomb, thou shalt not hold Him longer;
Death is strong, but Life is stronger;
Stronger than the dark, the light;
Stronger than the wrong, the right;
Faith and Hope triumphant say
Christ will rise on Easter Day.
—*Phillips Brooks, "An Easter Carol"*

* * *

'Twas Easter Sunday. The full blossomed trees
Filled all the air with fragrance and with joy.
—*Henry Wadsworth Longfellow, "The Spanish Student"*

D. LAW DAY

The law: It has honored me; may we honor it.
                    —*Daniel Webster, May 10, 1847*

* * *

The majesty and power of law and justice.
                    —*II Henry IV, V, 2*

* * *

May 1 is Law Day throughout the United States. It is a day when we pause to reflect on our duties as well as our rights as citizens.

It is fitting that our country has set aside one day each year to emphasize our respect for law, because ours is a nation which lives and prospers by law. We, the people, enjoy freedoms that exist no place else, because of our system and our protections.

We have the duty to obey the laws of the land;
   to respect the rights of others;
   to be informed on issues of government and community welfare;
   to vote in elections and to serve on juries if called;
   to serve and defend our country;
   and to assist agencies in law enforcement.
We also have the duty to practice and teach the principles of good citizenship in the home.
Our rights include: equal protection of laws and equal justice in the courts;
   to be free from arbitrary search and arrest;
   equal education and economic opportunity;
   the right to own property;
   the right to choose public officers in free elections;
   the right of free speech, press, and assembly, and to attend the church of our choice;
   the right to have legal counsel and prompt trial if accused of crime.   —*Sunshine Magazine*

E. MOTHER'S DAY

Where there is a mother in the house, matters speed well.
—*Amos Bronson Alcott, "Table Talk: Nurture"*

* * *

The mother's heart is the child's schoolroom.
—*Henry Ward Beecher, "Life Thoughts"*

* * *

Men are what their mothers made them.
—*Ralph W. Emerson, "Conduct of Life: Fate"*

* * *

All that I am my mother made me.—*John Quincy Adams*

* * *

All that I am or hope to be, I owe to my angel mother.
—*Attributed to Abraham Lincoln*

* * *

You may have tangible wealth untold;
Caskets of jewels and coffers of gold.
Richer than I you can never be—
I had a mother who read to me.
—*Strickland Gillilan, "The Reading Mother"*

* * *

Youth fades; love droops; the leaves of
friendship fall:
A mother's secret love outlives them all.
—*Oliver Wendell Holmes, "The Mother's Secret"*

* * *

This is a moment I deeply wish my parents could have lived
to share. In the first place my father would have enjoyed what
you have so generously said of me—and my mother would have
believed it.—*Lyndon B. Johnson, Commencement Address at
Baylor University, Waco, Texas, 28 May, 1965*

I pray that our Heavenly Father may assuage the anguish of your bereavement and leave you only the cherished memory of the loved and lost, and the solemn pride that must be yours to have laid so costly a sacrifice upon the altar of freedom. —*Abraham Lincoln, Letter, 21 November, 1864, to Mrs. Bixby of Boston, who lost five sons in the Civil War*

* * *

Mother's Day began to be observed about sixty years ago and was established by Presidential proclamation in 1914. But long before this, famous men of all ages have echoed in word and deed the proverb, "There is no mother like my mother."

Whistler called the painting of his mother "An Arrangement in Black and Gray." He objected to calling it "Mother" because he felt that his love for her was so sacred and personal that the rest of the world had no right to be sentimental about her.

Napoleon always stood in awe of his beautiful mother and often declared that she had the brains of a man. She managed everything with a prudence and sagacity which were incredible for her sex and age.

George Washington gave up all his hopes of being a sailor because his mother could not bear to have him leave her.

Lincoln was nine when his mother died. Her dying words were: "Be something, Abe."

Eugene Field was six when his mother died. But he said: "I have carried the remembrance of her gentle voice and soothing touch all through my life."

Carlyle wrote: "I am proud of Mother. If I ever forget to reverence her, I must cease to be a creature myself worth remembering."

Thomas Moore wrote to his mother twice a week, and at the time of her death, she possessed 4,000 of his letters.

John Quincy Adams every night of his life said the childish prayer, "Now I lay me down to sleep," that his mother had taught him.

Someone has said, "The mothers of famous men survive only in their sons." And in the words and deeds of these sons we have seen how everlastingly and beautifully they do survive.
—*Historical Data from Sunshine Magazine*

* * *

While the annual observance of Mother's Day is a time for honoring all mothers, it can also be a time for rededication on the part of mothers themselves, who often feel they lost their way in the maze of everyday duties and responsibilities. Here is a "Mother's Pledge," by an unknown author, that expresses this spirit of dedication of motherhood:

I will do my part to make our home a happy place of work, play, love, and worship.

I will keep a sense of humor and learn to laugh, even at myself, making it a habit to exercise my smiling muscles more and my tear ducts less.

I will give religion an important place in my heart and in our home, with definite time for Bible study, prayer, and family worship.

I will seek to understand and enjoy our children and to appreciate each one for what he is and for what he can do.

I will never punish to relieve my inner feelings but rather to bring good into the lives of our children.

I will lead them to an appreciation of beautiful literature, music, art, and the world of nature about us.

I will lead them to appreciate and befriend people of all races, to live above petty grievances and neighborhood gossip.

I will take time to read, talk, and listen to our children, and to answer honestly all their questions about life.

I will do all I can to prepare them for happy, useful living.
—*Sunshine Magazine*

* * *

While millions of modern mothers will again be honored on Mother's Day this year, few dutiful sons and daughters realize that Mom had her own special day several thousand years ago! According to historians, the early pagans of the Near East and Mediterranean regions worshipped an "Earth Mother" at annual woodland festivals.

In Asia Minor, a day was set aside for honoring Cybele, "Mother of the Gods." When the Romans adopted the festival and called it the "Feast of Hilaria," the whole family danced through the streets wearing garlands of leaves in their tresses.

Papa ruled the roost in most of Colonial America. But if early American settlers didn't set aside a special day for Mother, it wasn't because she wasn't highly esteemed. It was just that the strict Puritans didn't go in much for holidays of any kind.

In fact, Mother's Day wasn't celebrated anywhere in the United States until 1907. That year Anna M. Jarvis arranged a special church service in Grafton, West Virginia, to commemorate her own late mother and other mothers—living and deceased—of the community. Because the carnation was her mother's favorite flower, Anna Jarvis asked that each person attending the services wear a white carnation. Mother's Day was proclaimed a national holiday by President Woodrow Wilson in 1914.

You are mistaken if you fancy that the United States is the only country that has a day for honoring Mom. The English have been doing it for more than five hundred years with "Mothering Sunday"—the fourth Sunday in Lent—when they pay a special visit to their mothers, bearing candy, flowers, and little spiced cakes baked for the occasion.

According to information from the National Committee on the Observance of Mother's Day, the up-to-date version of the holiday is celebrated not only in the United States, but in far-flung places in Mexico, Canada, South America, China, Japan, and Africa!—*Sunshine Magazine*

F. MEMORIAL DAY

These heroes are dead. They died for liberty—they died for us. They are at rest. They sleep in the land they made free, under the flag they rendered stainless, under the solemn pines, the sad hemlocks, the tearful willows, the embracing vines. They sleep beneath the shadows of the clouds, careless alike of sunshine or storm, each in the windowless palace of rest. Earth may run red with other wars—they are at peace. In the midst of battles, in the roar of conflict, they found the serenity of death.—*Robert G. Ingersoll, Memorial Day Vision*

* * *

We have met on a great battlefield of that war. We have come to dedicate a portion of that field as a final resting-place for those who here gave their lives that that nation might live. It is altogether fitting and proper that we should do this. But in a larger sense, we cannot dedicate, we cannot consecrate, we cannot hallow this ground. The brave men, living and dead, who struggled here, have consecrated it far above our poor power to add or detract. The world will little note, nor long remember, what we say here, but it can never forget what they did here.—*Abraham Lincoln, Gettysburg Address, 19 Nov., 1863*

* * *

Old soldiers never die; they just fade away.
—*General Douglas MacArthur, Address to joint session of U. S. Congress, 19 April, 1951*

* * *

In my dreams I hear again the crash of guns, the rattle of musketry, the strange, mournful mutter of the battlefield. But in the evening of my memory, always I come back to West Point.
—*General Douglas MacArthur, Address at U. S. Military Academy, West Point, New York, 12 May, 1962*

* * *

My estimate of him (the American man-at-arms) was formed on the battlefield many, many years ago, and has never changed. I regarded him then as I regard him now—as one of the world's noblest figures . . . His name and fame are the birthright of every American citizen.—*General Douglas Mac-Arthur, Address at U. S. Military Academy, West Point, New York, 12 May, 1962*

* * *

The soldier, above all other people, prays for peace, for he must suffer and bear the deepest wounds and scars of war. —*General Douglas MacArthur, Address at U. S. Military Academy, West Point, New York, 12 May, 1962*

* * *

> The little green tents where the soldiers sleep
> and the sunbeams play and the women weep,
> Are covered with flowers today.
> —*Walt Mason, The Little Green Tents*

* * *

Here rests in honored glory an American soldier known but to God.—*Inscription on tomb of the Unknown Soldier, Arlington National Cemetery*

* * *

A state representative in Ohio got a letter from the local American Legion Post: "You are invited to be one of the speakers at our Memorial Day meeting. The program will include a talk by the Mayor, recitation of Lincoln's Gettysburg speech by a high school pupil, your talk, and then the firing squad."

G. FATHER'S DAY

Father's Day is the day we honor father and commend him for his job in building the character of young America.

Just as the family is the basic group in our republic, so is the individual the first basic unit. And each individual is the product of his father's guidance and teaching.

A few years ago the National Father's Day Committee suggested ten guideposts to a safe and better world, and a happy and peaceful family life:

The wise father—

—encourages a respect for other nations; an understanding of other peoples.

—gives his child confidence through the safety of a happy home.

—teaches his child that he is no better than others, despite any differences.

—is quick to offer a helping hand in times of trouble.

—schools his child in good sportsmanship and fair play—win, lose, or draw.

—gains respect and love of his child not by force but through companionship and wisdom.

—teaches his child the importance of good citizenship, by his own activity in community affairs.

—instills in his child a respect for law and order.

—teaches his child that intolerance and ignorance are alien to a world of peace.

—through spiritual guidance, teaches his child that greatness and goodness go hand in hand.

H. INDEPENDENCE DAY

O beautiful for patriot dream
That sees beyond the years
Thine alabaster cities gleam
Undimmed by human tears!
America! America!
God shed His grace on thee,
And crown thy good with brotherhood
From sea to shining sea!

—*Katharine Lee Bates*

* * *

Thou, too, sail on, O Ship of State!
Sail on, O Union, strong and great!
Humanity with all its fears,

With all the hopes of future years,
Is hanging breathless on thy fate!

—*Henry W. Longfellow*

* * *

Only those Americans who are willing to die for their country are fit to live.—*Douglas MacArthur*

* * *

I pledge allegiance to the flag of the United States and to the Republic for which it stands, one nation, indivisible with liberty and justice for all.

—*James B. Upham and Francis Bellamy*

* * *

American liberty is a religion. It is a thing of the spirit. It is an aspiration on the part of the people for not only a free life but a better life.—*Wendell L. Willkie*

* * *

The cause of freedom is the cause of God.—*Samuel Bowles*

* * *

Personal liberty is the paramount essential to human dignity and human happiness.—*Edward Bulwer-Lytton*

* * *

When Freedom from her mountain height
Unfurled her standard to the air,
She tore the azure robe of night,
And set the stars of glory there.

—*Joseph Rodman Drake*

* * *

For what avail the plough or sail,
Or land, or life, if freedom fail?

—*Ralph Waldo Emerson*

* * *

Ay, call it holy ground
The soil where first they trod;

They have left unstained, what there they found,—
Freedom to worship God.—*Felicia D. Hemans*

* * *

Many politicians are in the habit of laying it down as a self-evident proposition that no people ought to be free till they are fit to use their freedom. The maxim is worthy of the fool in the old story who resolved not to go into the water till he had learned to swim.—*Thomas B. Macaulay*

* * *

The only freedom which deserves the name is that of pursuing our own good in our own way, so long as we do not attempt to deprive others of theirs or impede their efforts to obtain it. —*John Stuart Mill*

* * *

Only free peoples can hold their purpose and their honor steady to a common end, and prefer the interests of mankind to any narrow interest of their own.—*Woodrow Wilson*

* * *

Yesterday the greatest question was decided which ever was debated in America; and a greater perhaps never was, nor will be, decided among men. A resolution was passed without one dissenting colony, that these United Colonies are, and of right ought to be, free and independent States.—*John Adams, Letter to Mrs. Adams*

* * *

It is my living sentiment, and by the blessing of God it shall be my dying sentiment,—Independence now and Independence forever!—*Daniel Webster, Eulogy in memory of John Adams and Thomas Jefferson, 2 August, 1826*

* * *

The United States is the only country with a known birthday.—*James G. Blaine, America's Natal Day*

* * *

That which distinguishes this day from all others is that it is when both orators and artillerymen shoot blank cartridges. —*John Burroughs, Journal, 4 July, 1859*

When in the course of human events, it becomes necessary for one people to dissolve the political bonds which have connected them with another, and to assume among the powers of the earth, the separate and equal station to which the laws of nature and of nature's God entitle them, a decent respect to the opinions of mankind requires that they should declare the causes which impel them to the separation.—*Thomas Jefferson, Declaration of Independence: Preamble*

* * *

We hold these truths to be self-evident, that all men are created equal, that they are endowed by their Creator with certain unalienable Rights, that among these are Life, Liberty and the pursuit of Happiness. That to secure these rights, Governments are instituted among Men, deriving their just powers from the consent of the governed. That whenever any Form of Government becomes destructive of these ends, it is the Right of the People to alter or to abolish it, and to institute new Government, laying its foundation on such principles and organizing its powers in such form, as to them shall seem most likely to effect their Safety and Happiness . . . We, therefore, . . . do . . . solemnly publish and declare, That these United Colonies are, and of Right ought to be free and independent States . . . And for the support of this Declaration, with a firm reliance on the protection of Divine Providence, we mutually pledge to each other our Lives, our Fortunes, and our sacred Honor.—*Thomas Jefferson, Declaration of Independence, as adopted by the Continental Congress, Philadelphia, 4 July, 1776*

* * *

Day of glory! Welcome day!
Freedom's banners greet thy ray.
   —*John Pierpont, "The Fourth of July"*

Jefferson's Declaration of Independence is a practical document for the use of practical men. It is not a thesis for philosophers, but a whip for tyrants; it is not a theory of government, but a program of action.—*Woodrow Wilson, Speech in Indianapolis, 13 April, 1911*

America! America!
God shed His grace on thee
And crown thy good with brotherhood
From sea to shining sea!
      —*Katharine Lee Bates, "America the Beautiful"*

* * *

O, Columbia, the gem of the ocean,
The home of the brave and the free,
The shrine of each patriot's devotion,
A world offers homage to thee.
—*Thomas à Becket, "Columbia, the Gem of the Ocean"*

* * *

Thou, too, sail on, O Ship of State!
Sail on, O Union, strong and great!
Humanity with all its fears,
With all the hopes of future years,
Is hanging breathless on thy fate! . . .
Sail on, nor fear to breast the sea!
Our hearts, our hopes, are all with thee,
Our hearts, our hopes, our prayers, our tears,
Our faith triumphant o'er our fears,
Are all with thee,—are all with thee!
—*Henry Wadsworth Longfellow, "The Building of the Ship"*

* * *

Driven from every other corner of the earth, freedom of thought and the right of private judgment in matters of conscience direct their course to this happy country as their last asylum.—*Samuel Adams*

* * *

Bring me men to match my mountains;
Bring me men to match my plains,—
Men with empires in their purpose,
And new eras in their brains.
      —*Sam Walter Foss, "The Coming American"*

This was the basic heritage of America—a heritage of tolerance, moderation, and individual liberty that was implanted from the very beginning of European settlement in the New World. America has quite rightly been called a nation that was "born free."—*J. W. Fulbright*

* * *

To embody human liberty in workable government, America was born.—*Herbert Hoover, Speech at Republican national convention, Cleveland, 10 June, 1936*

* * *

My God! How little do my countrymen know what precious blessings they are in possession of, and which no other people on earth enjoy!—*Thomas Jefferson, Letter to James Monroe, 17 June, 1785*

* * *

My most fervent prayer is to be a President who can make it possible for every boy in this land to grow to manhood by loving his country—instead of dying for it.—*Lyndon B. Johnson, Address in Washington, D.C., 24 March, 1964*

* * *

For this is what America is all about. It is the uncrossed desert and the unclimbed ridge. It is the star that is not reached and the harvest that's sleeping in the unplowed ground.
—*Lyndon B. Johnson, Inaugural Address, 20 January, 1965*

* * *

I believe in the United States of America as a government of the people, by the people, for the people; whose just powers are derived from the consent of the governed; a democracy in a republic; a sovereign nation of many sovereign states; a perfect union, one and inseparable; established upon those principles of freedom, equality, justice, and humanity for which American patriots sacrificed their lives and fortunes. I therefore believe it is my duty to my country to love it, to support its constitution, to obey its laws, to respect its flag, and to defend it against all enemies.—*William Tyler Page, The American's Creed*

* * *

Four freedoms . . . The first is freedom of speech and expression—everywhere in the world. The second is freedom of every person to worship God in his own way—everywhere in the world. The third is freedom from want . . . everywhere in the world. The fourth is freedom from fear . . . anywhere in the world.—*Franklin D. Roosevelt, Message to Congress, 6 January, 1941, proposing the lend-lease program. The substance of these aims, termed essential to the postwar world, was included in the Atlantic Charter, August, 1941*

* * *

Let our object be, our country, our whole country, and nothing but our country. And, by the blessing of God, may that country itself become a vast and splendid monument, not of oppression and terror, but of wisdom, of peace, and of liberty, upon which the world may gaze with admiration forever. —*Daniel Webster, Speech in Charlestown, Massachusetts, 17 June, 1825*

* * *

America is not anything if it consists of each of us. It is something only if it consists of all of us; and it can consist of all of us only as our spirits are banded together in a common enterprise. That common enterprise is the enterprise of liberty and justice and right.—*Woodrow Wilson, Speech in Pittsburgh, 29 January, 1916*

* * *

The fabulous country—the place where miracles not only happen, but where they happen all the time.—*Thomas Wolfe, "Of Time and the River"*

America is God's Crucible, the great Melting Pot where all the races of Europe are melting and re-forming! . . . God is making the American.—*Israel Zangwill, "The Melting-Pot"*

* * *

This, then, is the state of the union: free and restless, growing and full of hope. So it was in the beginning. So it shall always be, while God is willing, and we are strong enough to keep the faith.—*Lyndon B. Johnson, State of the Union message, 4 January, 1965*

* * *

Let us now join reason to faith, and action to experience, to transform our unity of interest into a unity of purpose. For the hour and the day and the time are here to achieve progress without strife, to achieve change without hatred; not without differences of opinion, but without the deep and abiding divisions which scar the Union for generations.—*Lyndon B. Johnson, Inaugural Address, 20 January, 1965*

* * *

Let us then stand by the constitution as it is, and by our country as it is, one, united, and entire; let it be a truth engraven on our hearts; let it be born on the flag under which we rally in every exigency, that we have one country, one constitution, one destiny.—*Daniel Webster, Speech in New York, 15 March, 1837*

* * *

Is life so dear or peace so sweet as to be purchased at the price of chains and slavery? Forbid it, Almighty God! I know not what course others may take; but as for me, give me liberty, or give me death!—*Patrick Henry, Speech in the Virginia House of Delegates, 23 March, 1775*

* * *

Listen, my children, and you shall hear,
Of the midnight ride of Paul Revere,
On the eighteenth of April, in seventy-five;

Hardly a man is now alive
Who remembers that famous day and year.
>—*Henry W. Longfellow, "Paul Revere's Ride"*

* * *

For scores of years I have been the banner of hope and freedom for generation after generation of Americans.

Born amid the first flames of America's fight for freedom, I am the symbol of a country that has grown from a little group of thirteen colonies to a united nation of fifty sovereign states. Planted firmly on the high pinnacle of American Faith my gently fluttering folds have proved an inspiration to untold millions.

Men have followed me into battle with unwavering courage. They have looked upon me as a symbol of national unity. They have prayed that they and their fellow citizens might continue to enjoy the life, liberty, and pursuit of happiness which have been granted to every American as the heritage of free men.

So long as men love liberty more than life itself; so long as they treasure the priceless privileges bought with the blood of our forefathers; so long as the principles of truth, justice, and charity for all remain deeply rooted in human hearts, I shall continue to be the enduring banner of the United States of America.

I Am Old Glory!

* * *

Upon this land a thousand, thousand blessings.—*Henry VIII*

* * *

I know no South, no North, no East, no West, to which I owe any allegiance.—*Henry Clay, Speech, 1848*

* * *

Our Federal Union; it must be preserved.—*Andrew Jackson, on Jefferson's birthday celebration, 1830*

* * *

That man's the best cosmopolite
Who loves his native country best.
>—*Alfred Tennyson, Hands All Around*

One flag, one land, one heart, one hand,
One nation, ever more!

—*O. W. Holmes, 1862*

* * *

In spite of the fact that the Declaration of Independence is one of the most famous public papers in the world it had no permanent home for more than a hundred years. Twice it barely escaped being destroyed by fire, and in both the Revolutionary War and the War of 1812 it just missed being captured by the British. Added to these narrow escapes was a nearly ruinous attempt to make a copperplate of it. In recent years it has been sealed in a glass-and-bronze case filled with inert helium gas in the National Archives Exhibition Hall in Washington, D.C. It can be lowered at a moment's notice into a large shockproof and fireproof safe.—*Sunshine Magazine*

* * *

The signers of the Declaration of Independence numbered fifty-six men. They were of varied backgrounds, ages, education, property, and experience. Some were already famous— Adams, Franklin; some were unheard of, recruited at the last minute as replacements for men who refused to support independence. Two of the signers were only twenty years of age; sixteen were in their thirties; twenty in their forties; eleven in their fifties; six in their sixties; and only one, Franklin, over seventy. All but two were married; each had an average of six children. Twenty-five were lawyers; twelve were merchants; four were doctors; one a preacher; and a famous one, a printer. Half were college graduates; some were self-educated. Few benefited from their bravery but not one recanted his original declaration of independence.—*Sunshine Magazine*

I. LABOR DAY

No one can do his work well who does not think it of importance.

What the country needs is dirtier fingernails and cleaner minds.—*Will Rogers*

* * *

Set it down as a fact to which there are no exceptions, that we must labor for all that we have, and nothing is worth possessing or offering to others, which costs us nothing.—*The Sunday School*

* * *

Labor disgraces no man: unfortunately man occasionally disgraces labor.—*Ulysses S. Grant*

* * *

On the whole, with scandalous exceptions, democracy has given the ordinary worker more dignity than he ever had. —*Sinclair Lewis*

* * *

He who prays and labours lifts his heart to God with his hands.—*St. Bernard*

* * *

A truly American sentiment recognizes the dignity of labor and the fact that honor lies in honest toil.—*(Stephen) Grover Cleveland*

* * *

The labor union is an elemental response to the human instinct for group action in dealing with group problems. —*William Green*

* * *

If little labour, little are our gains:
Man's fortunes are according to his pains.—*Robert Herrick*

* * *

Labor, if it were not necessary for the existence, would be indispensable for the happiness of man.—*Samuel Johnson*

* * *

If you want knowledge, you must toil for it; if food, you must toil for it; and if pleasure, you must toil for it: toil is the law.—*John Ruskin*

Labour was the first price, the original purchase money that was paid for all things.—*Adam Smith*

* * *

In every rank, of great or small,
'Tis industry supports us all.—*John Gay*

* * *

Labor is discovered to be the grand conqueror, enriching and building up nations more surely than the proudest battles.
—*William Ellery Channing, War*

* * *

There can be no distress, there can be no hard times, when labor is well paid. The man who raises his hand against the progress of the workingman raises his hand against prosperity.
—*W. Bourke Cockran, Speech in New York City, 18 August, 1896*

J. THANKSGIVING

When the Sunday school teacher asked her class what they were thankful for, one little fellow replied, "My glasses."

He explained, "They keep the boys from fighting me and the girls from kissing me."—*Together*

* * *

Gratitude: The memory of the heart.

* * *

If you have nothing to be thankful for, make up your mind that there is something wrong with you.

* * *

Thanksgiving is good, thanksliving is better.

* * *

Gratitude is not only the memory, but the homage of the heart—rendered to God for His goodness.—*N. P. Willis*

Father asked little Kathy if she didn't want to thank God for sending her such a fine new baby brother. Imagine his surprise when he heard this prayer: "Thank you, dear God, for Jimmy. I'm especially thankful that Jimmy wasn't twins like I heard the doctor say he might be."

* * *

A grateful mind is a great mind.

* * *

Be careful for nothing;
Be prayerful for everything;
Be thankful for anything.—*D. L. Moody*

* * *

He who thanks but with the lips
Thanks but in part;
The full, the true Thanksgiving
Comes from the heart.

* * *

The spirit of thanksgiving was defined by Carlyle when he said that a man should put himself at zero, and then reckon every degree ascending from that point as an occasion for thanks.

That is what those rugged forefathers of ours did, but it is not always what we today, who in America are the beneficiaries of all history's greatest bounties, do. Too often we are apt to complain, to look upon the dark side, to magnify the evils instead of the goodness with which we live.

But it is a truth that despite our century's wars, our difficulties, our fears, and our uncertainties, we live in a day of plenty and opportunity. We have more to be thankful for than almost any age in human history, and on this day let us remember that Thanksgiving Day is a "jewel, to set in the hearts of honest men," and be careful that we do not "take the day and leave out the gratitude."—*Sunshine Magazine*

Begger that I am, I am even poor in thanks.

—*William Shakespeare*

* * *

Heap high the board with plenteous
     cheer, and gather to the feast,
And toast the sturdy Pilgrim band
     whose courage never ceased.
Give praise to that All-Gracious One
     by whom their steps were led,
And thanks unto the harvest's Lord
     who sends our "daily bread."

—*Alice Williams Brotherton*

* * *

So once in every year we throng
Upon a day apart,
To praise the Lord with feast and song
In thankfulness of heart.—*Arthur Guiterman*

* * *

Ah! on Thanksgiving day, when
     from East and from West,
From North and South, come the
     pilgrim and guest.
When the gray-haired New Englander
     sees round his board
The old broken links of
     affection restored,
When the care-wearied man seeks
     his mother once more,
And the worn matron smiles where
     the girl smiled before.
What moistens the lips and what
     brightens the eye?
What calls back the past, like the
     rich pumpkin pie?—*John Greenleaf Whittier*

Thanksgiving Day . . . the one day that is purely American. —*O. Henry, "The Trimmed Lamp"; "Two Thanksgiving Day Gentlemen"*

* * *

Over three centuries ago, our forefathers in Virginia and in Massachusetts far from home in a lonely wilderness set aside a time for Thanksgiving.—*John F. Kennedy, Thanksgiving Proclamation, 5 November, 1963*

* * *

And let these altars, wreathed with flowers
And piled with fruits, awake again
Thanksgivings for the golden hours,
The early and the latter rain!
    —*John Greenleaf Whittier, "For an Autumn Festival"*

* * *

Give thanks unto the Lord, call upon his name, make known his deeds among the people.—*I Chronicles, 16, 8*

* * *

Give unto the Lord the glory due unto his name: bring an offering and come before him: worship the Lord in the beauty of holiness.—*I Chronicles, 16, 29*

* * *

O give thanks unto the Lord; for he is good; for his mercy endureth forever.—*I Chronicles, 16, 34*

* * *

Be thou exalted Lord, in thine own strength: so will we sing and praise thy power.—*Psalms, 21, 13*

* * *

Bless the Lord, O my soul, and forget not all his benefits. —*Psalms, 103, 2*

* * *

Great is the Lord, and greatly to be praised, and his greatness is unsearchable.—*Psalms, 145, 3*

* * *

The eyes of all wait upon thee; and thou givest them their meat in due season.—*Psalms, 145, 15*

Thou openest thine hand, and satisfiest the desire of every living thing.—*Psalms, 145, 16*

* * *

Make a joyful noise unto the Lord, all the earth; make a loud noise, and rejoice, and sing praise.—*Psalms, 98, 4*

* * *

Sing unto the Lord with the harp; with the harp, and the voice of a psalm.—*Psalms, 98, 5*

* * *

With trumpets and sound of cornet make a joyful noise before the Lord, the King.—*Psalms, 98, 6*

* * *

Honour the Lord with thy substance, and with the first-fruits of all thine increase.—*Proverbs 3, 9*

* * *

So shall thy barns be filled with plenty, and thy presses shall burst out with new wine.—*Proverbs 3, 10*

* * *

It is a good thing to give thanks unto the Lord, and to sing praises unto thy name, O most High.—*Psalms, 92, 1*

* * *

Offer unto God thanksgiving; and pay thy vows unto the most High.—*Psalms, 1, 14*

* * *

Let us come before his presence with thanksgiving, and make a joyful noise unto him with psalms.—*Psalms, 95, 2*

* * *

Being enriched in every thing to all bountifulness, which causeth through us thanksgiving to God.—*II Corinthians, 9, 11*

* * *

O Lord our heavenly Father . . . We praise Thee that Thou hast surrounded us with Thine infinite goodness, that Thou hast continually poured forth Thy benefits age after age, and that of Thy faithfulness there is no end. For the beauty of the earth, and the bounty it produces for our physical need, for the order and constancy of nature which brings us day and night, summer and winter, seedtime and harvest—for all gifts of Thy mercy—we are thankful.—*The Reverend Donald A. Wenstrom, "Pulpit Digest"*

* * *

As we approach this Thanksgiving let us pause to reflect upon the many many blessings that are ours. Blessings that we accept as commonplace—things that we feel are owed to us. We enjoy the highest standard of living in the world and we expect it. In the U.S. we have more homes owned by families, more autos, more television sets, more washing machines, more bath tubs—more of anything we can name than any place else on the face of the earth . . . So now, this Thanksgiving, it behooves all of us, on bended knee, to give thanks to Almighty God, for all the multitude of blessings He has showered upon each and every one of us, and pray that He will help us preserve our way of life.—*H. S. Jackson, "Indiana Freemason"*

* * *

We thank thee, O Lord, for the privilege of being a part of our U.S. We thank Thee for our forefathers who established a nation in which there would be liberty and justice for all. We firmly believe that more people enjoy freedom and more people share in opportunities here than anywhere else on earth. We would be thankful for the gift of life. On this national Thanksgiving Day, we are doubly grateful that you gave us the privilege of being American.—*Nuggets*

K. CHRISTMAS

The origin of the world's most widely known Christmas carol, "O Come, All Ye Faithful," was long hidden in mystery.

From the discovery of a manuscript by an English vicar, it now appears that the words were composed and set to music by John Francis Wade in 1744.

This is truly an international carol. Wade, an Englishman living in France, wrote the words in Latin. It was later known as the Portuguese Hymn. This may be because it was early used in the chapel of the Portuguese London embassy.

The song has been translated into 120 languages. Although more than forty English translations have been made, the best known today was done by Frederick Oakeley in 1852.

The majestic melody captured the imagination of Americans, and has seen service as a tune in other Christmas settings. Sung to the words of "How Firm a Foundation," it was a favorite of such national leaders as Theodore Roosevelt and Robert E. Lee.

Word-pictures are painted so clearly by the song that children dearly enjoy singing it. Many learn the Latin words, too, which begin "Adeste fideles—." Adult hearts around the world have been stirred by this melody, expressing the triumphant message of the Incarnation.

O come, all ye faithful, joyful and triumphant,
O come ye, O come ye to Bethlehem.
Come and behold Him, born the King of Angels.

Sing, choirs of angels, sing in exultation,
Sing all ye citizens of Heav'n above:
Glory to God, all glory in the highest.

O come, let us adore Him, O come, let us adore Him.
O come, let us adore Him, Christ, the Lord.

—Sunshine Magazine

* * *

Hushed was the night and dark the hearts of men, as long ago the earth in slumber lay; the shepherds and the Wise Men of the East alone looked for the dawning of the day. But on that night there rose from out of the east a star whose radiant light and beauty rare shed beams of hope and love on lost mankind, and with hosannas filled the midnight air.

The darkest night is not without its star, the hopeless hours are oft before the dawn; the travail and the pangs of life's long years must come before eternal hope is born.

Long has man struggled on toward the dawn, and searched with tear-stained eyes for break of day; long has creation travailed, prayed, and yearned for earth's dark night of sin to pass away.

But now the sound of battle and of strife will soon from east to west be made to cease, and nations all in silent awe behold the coming of the mighty Prince of Peace.—*Sunshine Magazine*

* * *

If you hitch your wagon to a star, be sure it is the Star of Bethlehem.

* * *

Little Janie was being taught that it was proper to write a "thank you" letter to those persons who sent her gifts at Christmas. She seemed to do well until it came to Aunt Martha's gift. Finally she finished her note which read: "Thank you for your Christmas present. I always wanted a pin-cushion, although not very much."

* * *

Christmas living is the best kind of Christmas giving. —*Henry van Dyke*

* * *

The Christmas spirit that goes out with the dried-up Christmas tree is just as worthless.—*Fred Beck*

* * *

Retail merchants who share in billions of Christmas business will tell you emphatically that there is a Santa Claus. —*George Washburn*

* * *

I sometimes think we expect too much of Christmas Day. We try to crowd into it the long arrears of kindliness and humanity of the whole year.—*David Grayson*

The first Christmas that little Jane learned to read she was allowed to distribute the family gifts on Christmas eve. According to the family custom, the one who distributed the gifts could open the first package. After all the gifts were distributed with loving care, Jane kept looking around the tree and among its branches. Finally father asked, "What are you looking for, dear?"

To which Jane replied, "I thought Christmas was Jesus' birthday and I was just wondering where His present is. I guess everyone forgot Him."

* * *

In the Austrian Tyrol nestles the remote town of Obendorf. Joseph Mohr was the devout priest of the town; Franz Xavier Gruber, his friend, was the village choirmaster and church organist. Both were lovers of music. The two men had often agreed that the perfect Christmas song had not yet been found. Meditating on this thought, Mohr sat in his study on Christmas eve, 1818. Outside the air was still and cold. Suddenly, thoughts which had been forming in Mohr's mind found clear expression: Stille Nacht, heilige Nacht.

The next morning Mohr hurried to his friend's home with the manuscript. Gruber then composed the music. Gruber exclaimed with joy in his heart as he sang it for the first time, "It sings itself, young son." Later in the evening they sang their new song before their first audience. The little company of auditors thanked their two friends with tears and joy in their eyes.

Tradition says that the song lay on Gruber's desk for a year. Then it was tried on the church organ. The organ builder was so entranced that he begged to take a copy to a little town across the mountain. There it was sung by four sisters by the name of Strasser. This song became the favorite of the "Strasser quartet." They were invited to sing the hymn in the cathedral of Leipzig. It became known as the "Tyrolean Song."

It was first honored in 1854 when a full choir sang it in the imperial church of Berlin before Emperor Frederich Wilhelm IV. Thereafter it was ordered to have first place in all Christmas programs. The English version:

>Silent night, holy night,
>All is calm, all is bright,
>'Round yon Virgin, Mother and Child,
>Holy infant, so tender and mild,
>Sleep in heavenly peace.
>>—*Clyde D. Foster in Chicago Tribune*

* * *

I heard the bells on Christmas Day
Their old, familiar carols play,
With wild and sweet
The words repeat
Of peace on earth, good-will to men!—*Longfellow*

* * *

For unto you is born this day in the city of David a Saviour, which is Christ the Lord.—*Luke II: 11*

* * *

Let's dance and sing and make good cheer.
For Christmas comes but once a year.—*G. MacFarren*

* * *

>'Twas the night before Christmas,
>when all through the house
>Not a creature was stirring—
>not even a mouse;
>The stockings were hung by the
>chimney with care,
>In hopes that St. Nicholas soon
>would be there.—*Clement C. Moore*

* * *

>O little town of Bethlehem,
>How still we see thee lie!
>Above thy deep and dreamless sleep
>The silent stars go by.—*Phillips Brooks*

On Christmas morning I was telling the story of the Nativity to a group of junior boys in my Sunday School class. To test their attentiveness, I began to ask questions. Expecting a reply of either "the shepherds" or "the Wise Men," I asked, "Who was the first to know of Jesus' birth?"

Immediately a small lad waved his hand and shouted, "Mary!"

* * *

Hark the herald angels sing,
"Glory to the new-born king."
Peace on earth, and mercy mild,
God and sinners reconciled!—*Charles Wesley*

* * *

Blow, bugles of battle, the marches of peace;
East, west, north, and south let the long quarrel cease;
Sing the song of great joy that the angels began,
Sing the glory of God and of goodwill to man!
—*John Greenleaf Whittier*

* * *

Not believe in Santa Claus! You might as well not believe in fairies . . . Nobody sees Santa Claus, but that is no sign that there is no Santa Claus. The most real things in the world are those which neither children nor men can see. No Santa Claus! Thank God! He lives and he lives forever.

Francis P. Church, "Is There a Santa Claus?" This famous editorial, which originally appeared in the New York Sun, 21 Sept., 1897, was in reply to a child, Virginia O'Hanlon, whose faith had been shaken by skeptical playmates.

"Yes, Virginia, there is a Santa Claus. He exists as certainly as love and generosity and devotion exist." —*Francis P. Church, "Is There a Santa Claus?"; New York Sun, 21 Sept., 1897*

Most of the time, the whole year round,
there ain't no flies on me,
But jest 'fore Christmas I'm as good as I
kin be!—*Eugene Field "Jest 'fore Christmas"*

* * *

There's a song in the air!
There's a star in the sky!
There's a mother's heart forlorn,
In every house the Christ is born.
—*Richard Watson Gilder, "A Madonna of Fra Lippo Lippi"*

* * *

It came upon the midnight clear,
That glorious song of old.
—*Edmund Hamilton Sears, "Christmas Carols"*

L. BIRTHDAY

In youth we clothe ourselves with rainbows, and go as
brave as the zodiac. In age, we put out another sort of perspiration—gout, fever, rheumatism, caprice, doubt, fretting, avarice.
—*Ralph W. Emerson, "Conduct of Life: Fate"*

* * *

Youth is the time for the adventures of the body, but age
for the triumphs of his mind.—*Logan Pearsall Smith, "On Reading Shakespeare"*

* * *

Of middle age the best that can be said is that a middle-
aged person has likely learned how to have a little fun in spite
of his troubles.—*Don Marquis, "The Almost Perfect State"*

* * *

Among the peaceful harvest days,
An Indian Summer comes at last!
—*Adeline D. T. Whitney, "Equinoctial"*

To me, old age is always fifteen years older than I am.
—*Bernard M. Baruch, upon observing his 85th birthday, in 1955*

* * *

Age . . . is a matter of feeling, not of years.—*George William Curtis, "Prue and I"*

* * *

I am long on ideas, but short on time. I expect to live to be only about a hundred.—*Thomas A. Edison, Golden Book, April, 1931*

* * *

The older I get, the more wisdom I find in the ancient rule of taking first things first—a process which often reduces the most complex human problems to manageable proportions. —*Dwight D. Eisenhower, "Let's Be Honest with Ourselves"; The Reader's Digest, December, 1963*

* * *

I'm saving that rocker for the day when I feel as old as I really am.—*Dwight D. Eisenhower*

* * *

We do not count a man's years, until he has nothing else to count.—*Ralph W. Emerson "Society and Solitude: Old Age"*

* * *

All would live long, but none would be old.—*Benjamin Franklin, "Poor Richard," 1749*

* * *

Many foxes grow gray, but few grow good.—*Benjamin Franklin, "Poor Richard," 1749*

* * *

Old boys have their playthings as well as young ones; the difference is only in the price.—*Benjamin Franklin, "Poor Richard," 1752*

Spring still makes spring in the mind
When sixty years are told;
Love makes anew this throbbing heart,
And we are never old.
Over the winter glaciers
I see the summer glow,
As through the wind-piled snowdrift,
The warm rosebuds below.
—*Ralph W. Emerson, "The World-Soul"*

* * *

And if I should live to be
The last leaf upon the tree
In the spring,
Let them smile, as I do now,
At the old forsaken bough
Where I cling.
—*Oliver Wendell Holmes, "The Last Leaf"*

* * *

The older I grow the more I distrust the familiar doctrine
that age brings wisdom.—*H. L. Mencken, "Prejudices"*

* * *

Call him not old whose visionary brain
Holds o'er the past its undivided reign.
For him in vain the envious seasons roll
Who bears eternal summer in his soul.
—*Oliver Wendell Holmes, "The Old Player"*

* * *

Youth longs and manhood strives, but age remembers,
Sits by the raked-up ashes of the past,
Spreads its thin hand above the whitening embers
That warm its creeping life-blood till the last.
—*Oliver Wendell Holmes, "The Iron Gate"*

* * *

It is too late! Ah, nothing is too late
Till the tired heart shall cease to palpitate.

Cato learned Greek at eighty; Sophocles
Wrote his grand Oedipus, and Simonides
Bore off the prize of verse from his compeers,
When each had numbered more than fourscore years, . . .
Chaucer, at Woodstock with the nightingales,
At sixty wrote the Canterbury Tales;
Goethe at Weimar, toiling to the last,
Completed Faust when eighty years were past.
These are indeed exceptions; but they show
How far the gulf-stream of our youth may flow
Into the arctic regions of our lives . . .
For age is opportunity no less
Than youth itself, though in another dress,
And as the evening twilight fades away
The sky is filled with stars, invisible by day.
          —*Henry W. Longfellow, "Morituri Salutamus"*

* * *

As life runs on, the roads grow strange
With faces new, and near the end
The milestones into headstones change,
'Neath every one a friend.
          —*J. R. Lowell, "Sixty-eighth Birthday"*

* * *

I promise to keep on living as though I expected to live
forever. Nobody grows old by merely living a number of
years. People grow old only by deserting their ideals. Years
may wrinkle the skin, but to give up interest wrinkles the soul.
—*General Douglas MacArthur, Address at the dedication of
the MacArthur Monument, Los Angeles, 26 January, 1955*

* * *

Pick the right grandparents, don't eat or drink too much,
be circumspect in all things, and take a two-mile walk every
morning before breakfast.—*Harry S Truman, Prescription for
reaching the age of 80. He made the statement to reporters in
Washington, May 8, 1964, on his own 80th birthday, and said he
hoped to live to be 90, but only "if the old think-tank is working."*

Past my next milestone waits my seventieth year.
I mount no longer when the trumpets call;
My battle-harness idles on the wall,
The spider's castle, camping-ground of dust,
Not without dints, and all in front, I trust.
—*James Russell Lowell, "Epistle to George William Curtis: Postscript," 1887*

* * *

Old Age, on tiptoe, lays her jeweled hand
Lightly on mine.
—*George Santayana, "A Minuet on Reaching the Age of Fifty."*

* * *

Oh! be thou blest with all that Heaven can send,
Long health, long youth, long pleasure—and a friend.
—*Alexander Pope*

M. WEDDING BREAKFAST, LUNCHEON OR DINNER

Go with me
To bless this twain that they may prosperous be.
—*Tempest, IV, I*

* * *

Now all the blessings of a glad father compass thee about!
—*Tempest, V, I*

* * *

Look down, you gods,
And on this couple drop a blessed crown!
—*Tempest, V, I*

* * *

But blest with her, 'tis spring throughout the year!
—*Alexander Pope*

* * *

Having such a blessing in his lady,
He finds the joys of Heaven here on earth.
—*Merchant of Venice, III, 5*

* * *

The Lord bless you! God prosper your affairs!
—*II Henry IV, III, 2*

CHAPTER 7

INTRODUCING THE SPEAKER

It is my pleasure and indeed a great honor to present a man in whose capable hands, in a very large measure, is the hope of the world for peace, the United States Secretary of State, the Honorable Dean Rusk.—*Richard T. Cragg introduces the Secretary of State*

* * *

Being a daring critic has many times brought disfavor and lawsuits. I am reminded of the delightful story about Heywood Broun the outstanding New York theatre critic whose reviews were usually gentle and encouraging.

However, one evening he attended a bad performance of an actor named Geoffrey Steyne. In his column he commented that Mr. Steyne was the worst actor on the American Stage. Mr. Steyne sued. The whole principle of dramatic criticism was at stake so the case was dismissed.

Broun's readers could hardly wait for his review of Goeffrey Steyne's next stage appearance. When this occurred, they eagerly turned to his review and to their dismay he did not mention Mr. Steyne until the very last sentence when he stated, "Mr. Steyne's performance was not up to his usual standard." —*From an introduction by Richard T. Cragg*

* * *

Our guest speaker today has been referred to as a "David Against the Goliaths of Industry." His charges against the safety standards of the automobile manufacturers has indeed stirred up a national controversy which will have a continuing effect over the next several years. Of course, the human element can upset all safety standards if the driver decides to speed. You remember the story told by Bennet Cerf, of the wealthy grain merchant who bought a new car and was enjoying his first ride in it no end until a motorcycle cop stopped him and suggested a visit to the local magistrate.

"He was doing sixty," reported the cop. "Nonsense," declared the merchant. "I never got her up above forty." The merchant's wife put in her two cents worth at this point. "He wasn't going faster than twenty-five," she argued. A friend who had been riding in the back seat added, "I'd say we were virtually at a standstill when this officer came along." The magistrate threw up his hands and cried, "Stop right now, before you folks back into something."

More recently Mr. Nader has blasted the safety standards of the gas and oil pipelines—another industrial giant. This, too, will be front page news for some time to come.—*From an introduction by Richard T. Cragg*

* * *

A few weeks ago during our more than normal snow problems, we had the United States Meteorologist in charge of Chicago at our speaker's table and when introduced he received a loud round of booing. Now as we approach the April 15 deadline for filing of income tax, I hope that we will refrain from any show of emotion when I introduce our guest speaker.

Many brilliant, well-meaning men find themselves involved in doing an outstandingly good job for our country in what might be considered an unpopular field. History tells us that through the ages, the tax collector has never won many popularity contests.

In fact many books have been written on humorous letters sent to the Internal Revenue Service. One that I have enjoyed was edited by Bill Adler last year with such letters as:

"In reply to an inquiry from his Internal Revenue District, one puzzled citizen wrote back—as far as I can determine, I never engaged any Internal Revenue Service. Will you kindly explain the transaction to which your recent form letter referred?"

"Sir: If these answers will not do, please schedule an inquest at your nearest local office."

A taxpayer who had several arguments over the years with his Internal Revenue Service wrote in after a lengthy lull:

"After many months of peaceful coexistence, I suppose we are both ready to resume our battle."

One district director received a reply from a taxpayer who had failed to file an information return. Scrawled across the form was the statement:

"I have been dead for almost a year."

Another one wrote:

"Sir; Tell Mr. Johnson, no more income tax cuts. I couldn't afford this one."—*Richard T. Cragg introduces the U. S. Commissioner of Internal Revenue, Sheldon S. Cohen*

* * *

I want to thank you, Mr. President, for that wonderful introduction. I am sure one of my assistants must have written it.

You perhaps think it was too elaborate. You perhaps heard the story of the young boy in the Texas League—small college league in north Texas—who had a very distinguished record as a football player; and when he finished he decided to go down to Houston and see one of the scouts of the pros to get a job.

The scout said, "I understand you have had a marvelous record."

The boy said, "Yes, I believe I have."

He asked, "Well, how did you do in football?"

He said, "I was a triple-threat man."

He asked, "How did you do in passing?"

He said, "I led the league in all history, 792 completions."

He asked, "How did you do in running?"

He said, "I hate to brag about it, but I had 14.7 yards every carry for four straight years."

He asked, "How did you do in your kicking?"

He said, "73.7 yards every time I kicked a ball."

"Well," the pro said, "that's really a magnificent record. What is your weakness?"

He said, "They say I am inclined to exaggerate."—*Roger D. Branigin, then Governor of Indiana, closes an address*

* * *

Before I introduce our key speaker, let me say that he has graciously offered to answer questions following his talk.

Our speaker today has shown remarkable leadership and outward calm in the face of a year long controversy critical to the future of his organization.

This surgeon and physician has led his colleagues wisely and compassionately through the perils of federal legislation to which many of his members were opposed, and he has healed the divided opinions within the ranks of his members on ethical issues.

As the new president, he quickly took a personal stand, a total personal commitment, in regard to citizenship and ethics, placing first in consideration the care which patients receive.

Those of us who know his background well, recognize that this man's skill in fellowship through the years has resulted in his present skill in leadership.

Due to this family doctor, the American Medical Association is headed boldly and bravely in a new direction. His organization now works closely with the Department of Health, Education and Welfare on the rules and regulations of the Medicare Program.

A distinguished Pennsylvanian, our speaker is the youngest elder statesman in American medicine. Dr. Percy Hopkins, Board Chairman of the American Medical Association says "He is the most knowledgeable man in organized medicine today."

Our speaker has led organized medicine through its most trying hours. Thinking ahead, as is his practice, he will lead us in our thinking today as he speaks on "New Experiments in Medical Care."

I present to you the right man, in the right place, at the right time. The greatest leader American medicine has ever had—James Z. Appel, Dr. Appel.—*Robert L. Lasater introduces Dr. James Z. Appel, then President of the American Medical Association*

* * *

To find a politician who, for twenty years, has never lost an election is rare indeed; but in modern times to find a Republican in New York City who usually receives a plurality vote, is unprecedented. A possible explanation for this phenomenon was offered by a New York Times writer, who said, "In Javits the swelling ranks of independents find a man who is intelligent, broad ranging in his interests, articulate, bluntly honest, hardworking and up to date."

On a typical day, the Senator is at the House gym at 8 a.m. when it opens—the Senate gym doesn't open until 10—too late for him. He spends the morning in his office and at noon, "as though guided by an automatic homing device," he is on his way to the floor. Whereas only a major issue will draw more than a few Senators, Javits is there to bedevil his colleagues whose only wish is to read a speech into the record without challenge. A friend has said that he envisions himself the conscience of the Senate, which is fortunate for us, because the GOP has only had a majority in four of his seventeen years in Congress.

As the son of immigrants and born on New York's Lowest East Side—which he has called an urban counterpart to a log cabin—our guest has often been asked why he is a Republican. In his most recent book he says, "Initially, I was attracted to the Republican Party for a highly personal reason that had nothing to do with any high sense of mission in national or international affairs. It had everything to do with certain personal experiences I had with local government in New York City.

"I remember, for example, how a day or two before an election my father—who worked full time as the janitor for three large tenements at a high of $45 a month, plus rooms—would walk a few blocks to a corner saloon, the proprietor of which was the local Democratic precinct captain, to load up on beer and free lunch. There, too, he would get $2 for each voter in his three tenement buildings, and as an honest man he would promptly distribute the allotment to the voters in question."

Gentlemen, it is my honor to present this outstanding Republican, Senator Javits.—*Donald Erickson introduces Senator Javits*

* * *

Our guest today has enjoyed a career of such broad dimensions that it encompasses activities and board directorships ranging from the Western Hemisphere to the Orient. Among his most recent and distinguished positions Ambassador Linowitz has served as Chairman of the National Committee on International Development, Chairman of the State Department's Advisory Committee on International Organizations and Chairman of the Board, Chairman of the Executive Committee and General Counsel for the Xerox Corporation, Director of Rank-Xerox, Ltd., London, and Fugi Limited, Japan. He has given equal attention to civic commitments, serving as director of the United Jewish Welfare Fund, board member of the John F. Kennedy Center for the Performing Arts, and on the Board of Managers of the Eastman School of Music, to give but a brief account.

As our Ambassador to the OAS he has been intimately involved with our policy toward Latin America and our activities there. His vast experience and understanding of world social and economic problems will be shared with us in his discussion of recent developments in Latin America and their significance for United States policy.

Ambassador Linowitz.—An introduction of Ambassador Sol Myron Linowitz to the Chicago Committee of the Chicago Council on Foreign Relations by Herbert V. Prochnow

* * *

Our speaker today is a venturesome man. He will talk to us on views which the President will hold in 1968 on national and international issues. For this undertaking he has remarkable qualifications. He has had more than twenty years in newscasting. He has traveled throughout much of the world. He has had his own well-known news program in Chicago. He has been anchorman on ABC News presentations on such varied subjects as "Free Press, Fair Trial" and "The Middle East War." He has done a special documentary study on Vietnam.

And for the past three years he has served ABC News as its White House Correspondent. In this capacity he has covered the President's goings not only in Washington and at the LBJ Ranch, but also in Glassboro when the President met Premier Kosygin, at Ponte del Este, when the President met with heads of state of the Organization of American States, and in South Vietnam, Korea and the Philippines.

In addition to all this, we welcome him as a longtime friend of the Council on Foreign Relations; and winner of its World Understanding Award.

I take great pleasure in presenting Mr. Frank Reynolds.

Mr. Reynolds . . . *—Herbert V. Prochnow introduces a Distinguished News Correspondent*

* * *

Today it is our great honor to have as our speaker Dr. Alberto Yeras Comargo, a former president of Colombia and one of Latin America's most respected and capable spokesmen. For four decades his work and efforts have demonstrated a deep and unswerving commitment to the cause of democratic government and economic and social progress in his own country and throughout Latin America. He has been associated with and often responsible for many of the institutions and programs that we find hopeful in Latin America today. In the course of his distinguished career he received numerous distinctions and honors, but perhaps the most significant of these is the respect and admiration not only of his countrymen, but also of people throughout this hemisphere who advocate progress and reforms by democratic methods.

Dr. Lleras began his career as a journalist, a profession which he still practices today. In the late 1920s, however, he began to take an active role in Colombia's Liberal party. He was elected to the national legislature in 1930, and was appointed Minister of the Interior in 1935 at the age of 29. He served the Liberal government in many capacities during the following year.

In 1945 he was elected by the Colombian Congress to serve out the remainder of the term of office of President Lopez who had resigned. In 1947 he was elected director-general of the Pan-American-Union and in 1948 Secretary-General of the Organization of American States, a position which he occupied until 1954 when he returned to Colombia as the president of the then new University of Los Andes.

His efforts during the next three years were especially important in Colombian history. Dr. Lleras was instrumental in arranging the agreement which ended the strife between the Liberal and Conservative parties and led eventually to the restoration of civilian government. He was inaugurated as President in 1958. The following four years were marked by a speedy restoration of freedoms which had been curtailed by the previous military government and by the ending of the civil strife which had plagued the country. In addition, a program of economic and social reforms and a commitment to the furtherance of economic and social progress was adopted which has been carried forward by successor governments.

In recent years he had been closely associated with the Alliance for Progress and other similar efforts in Latin America.

It is a very great pleasure for me to present the Honorable Dr. Alberto Yeras Comargo.—*Herbert V. Prochnow introduces a Foreign Government Statesman*

* * *

About three decades ago, a Denver teen-ager shouldered his way to the front of a holiday crowd gathered to christen the brand new Denver Zephyr as it entered service for the Burlington Railroad between Chicago and Denver. He remembers thinking, "This shiny train is really going to start something."

How right he was! The diesel age in railroading was underway, and though he may not have realized it at the time, the career of that teen-ager was underway right along with it. We are deeply honored to have him on our platform today.

His railroad career began when he served as a messenger for the Union Pacific while attending Denver University. These were depression years and jobs were scarce, but he learned telegraphy in his spare time and landed an assignment in Tulsa as a telegrapher for the St. Louis & San Francisco Railway.

Within a year he was a dispatcher, and then, successively, assistant trainmaster, trainmaster, superintendent, and vice president of the Frisco Line. He was then named president of the road and chairman.

Later he was named president of another great railroad, the Chicago, Burlington & Quincy, and we in the Middle West quickly began hearing exciting things about this "hard driving wheel of the Burlington."

Then another challenge beckoned, and he became president of the Northern Pacific, where he is giving the same imaginative leadership which marked his earlier presidencies.

He has brought energy and initiative to his tasks, spearheading drives for new industry and freight tonnage for each of the roads he has headed.

It is a very great privilege to present to this audience an outstanding railroader and corporate leader—a dynamic and talented business executive and civic leader—the president of the Northern Pacific Railroad—Mr. Louis Menk.—*Introduction of Louis W. Menk, President, Northern Pacific Railway Company by Dr. Duncan Wimpress, President, Monmouth College*

* * *

The career of our distinguished guest as a foreign Service Officer, culminating now in more than four years as our Ambassador to France, has extended over a period of thirty-five years and the administrations of six Presidents. In a service so long and so distinguished, some of the responsibilities that have fallen on him can be suggested—but only suggested—by the positions or the work which have engaged him.

Early in his career he served in Prague, Moscow and Tokyo, followed by internment; then Chief of the State Department's Division of Eastern European Affairs during the War; the Conferences of Moscow and Teheran in 1943, Dumbarton Oaks in 1944, and San Francisco and Moscow in 1945. He was Adviser to the United States delegation to the United Nations; twice Counsellor to the Department of State; Ambassador to Russia and Ambassador to the Philippines. He exemplifies the highest tradition of the Foreign Service and speaks from an extraordinary breadth of experience. He has agreed to answer questions following his remarks. We are honored to have Ambassador Charles E. Bohlen with us.

Mr. Ambassador.—*Herbert V. Prochnow introducing an American Ambassador*

* * *

It would be entirely inappropriate for me to give this audience of his friends and neighbors biographical data about as well known an Illinois citizen as Senator Percy.

Our guest today is in fact a fellow member of this organization and a member also of that body of one hundred men whose special distinction it is that without their concurrence there can be no laws of the United States, and without their advice and consent no treaties.

Only recently he has returned from a fact-gathering trip to Vietnam.

To his talk today on "Current Directions in U. S. Foreign Policy" he brings the authority of his position, the breadth of his experience, and the qualities of mind and character which mark him as a distinguished leader in his many areas of endeavor.

We are honored to welcome our fellow member and eminent Senator from Illinois, Charles H. Percy, who has also generously consented to answer questions following his remarks. Senator Percy.—*Herbert V. Prochnow introducing an American Senator*

* * *

In introducing our speaker today, I am reminded of an observation that has been made from time to time by one of our favorite Illinois institutions, Senator Everett McKinley Dirksen. It goes something like this:

(Imitating Senator Dirksen's voice) "In political campaigns one element ranks in importance above all others. It is the grist for the mill of the democratic process. It is that precious commodity whose presence is so essential if virtue is to triumph—money."

Our speaker today is one of the world's foremost experts on Senator Dirksen's favorite commodity. Our speaker is no stranger to the business, academic, and financial communities of this town or this nation.

He is, frankly, one of the most outstanding economists of our times—outstanding and outspoken. But even more, he is an outstanding American. He was an advisor to both Presidents Franklin Roosevelt and Lyndon Johnson, and when in this capacity he found himself in disagreement either with our nation's economic policy, or with the political policy which in his judgment has an over-all adverse effect on the nation's economic welfare, he has been honest, courageous, and tough enough to defend his position irrespective of the consequences.

His most recent book is entitled, "The Economics of Crisis." I commend it to you.

This then is no ordinary economist, no ordinary forecaster, and no ordinary man.—*Martin Koldyke Introduces Eliot Janeway*

* * *

President Jacobs: Gentlemen, it gives me great pleasure to present the Governor of Illinois, the Honorable Richard B. Ogilvie.

GOVERNOR RICHARD B. OGILVIE:

Gentlemen and distinguished guests: The privilege of addressing this forum is one that I prize highly. Few groups in this state have the prestige you have won through the years by your selection of the most sought-after speakers of the day.

Judging by some of the mail I have received recently, a lot of people are after me, too. I'm just grateful that most of the teabags I'm receiving are unused. There's a place for them in the economy program at the Executive Mansion.

Now the reason I prize this opportunity today is that it gives me a chance to say publicly to you, and to Illinois citizens generally, that I do not blame anyone for being concerned about my tax proposals.

But I reiterate today: those proposals are realistic. They are fair. And what's more, they are constitutional.

Some critics of the budget message have already talked of adding "sweetners" to the fiscal prescription for Illinois— sweetners that would make it more palatable to various groups and to taxpayers generally. To that, I say "fine"—if they can do it.

If they can meet the bedrock needs of this state, if they can discover a way that is both painless and constitutional, if they can come to grips with the problems we face without calling for some sacrifice by taxpayers—then I am all for them. But I have not seen or heard any adequate alternative plan.

In studying and planning the measures I proposed, the budget staff and I found we had a choice which we concluded was actually no choice at all.

For the choice was between responsible and honorable leadership on one hand, and shabby evasion of our duty, on the other hand.—*The President of the Executives Club of Chicago, Wyatt Jacobs, introduces the Governor of the State of Illinois who responds*

CHAPTER 8

OPENING AND CLOSING A SPEECH

A. OPENING A SPEECH

Dr. Roy Menninger opens an address on "The Dilemma of the Generations."

Distinguished fellows at this table, guests and members of this most distinguished club: I must confess to you a few moments of utter and total embarrassment as I recover from such a magnificent and stirring introduction.

These comments have been on my mind for some time and I have had the opportunity of sharing them with groups in other places and I find it a particularly welcome occasion to have this opportunity of sharing them with you.

There is nothing new in the observation that youth and age gaze at each other across a gap of suspicion, doubt, and hostility. Five centuries before Christ, Socrates bitterly attacked youth's "bad manner, contempt for authority, and disrespect for their elders," and declared that "children nowadays are tyrants." As one recent essayist put it, "All through history, denouncing the young has been a tonic for tired blood, and more important, defying elders is hygienic for the young.' Perhaps because the memory of the postwar "apathetic generation" of young is still quite vivid for most of us, the present strife between generations is all the more dramatic and dismaying.

* * *

John A. Barr, Dean of the Graduate School of Business Administration, Northwestern University begins an address.

For a businessman to talk with a group of health professionals may raise a question of whether we can communicate effectively. I think that we can, but I am reminded of the story of the church meeting that was being held one day. All of the members of the church were there to consider a proposal that the church buy a chandelier. One member arose and voiced very strong opposition. He said, "In the first place, there is no one in the church can spell it, and in the second place, there isn't a single member of the church that can play it. What we really need in this church are some lighting fixtures."

I am very happy to have this opportunity to participate in this Institute. I am happy to be here, not so much because planning is in vogue—although most everyone knows that planning is the thing to do these days—but rather because planning, and particularly organized long-range planning, is both important and essential if we are to achieve our objective of efficient and effective optimum health service.

* * *

Dr. John T. Middleton, Commissioner of the National Air Pollution Control Administration begins an address.

As a former Californian and native-born Chicagoan, I probably arrive here with some of California's parochial ideas. Californians like to think of the State of California as being one of the most beautiful, one of the larger ones, with the most beautiful trees, a big airplane business—and some of the most polluted air in the land.

But perhaps most of you do not realize that California is really the only state in the nation where one wakes up in the morning and hears the birds cough.

A few weeks ago at a meeting in Washington the National Wildlife Federation reported on the results of a nationwide poll conducted on its behalf by the Gallup organization to determine the attitude of the American public toward protecting our environment. It came as no suprise to me to learn that the public is deeply concerned about the environment—in fact, sufficiently concerned that the majority of those interviewed indicated they would be willing to pay more taxes to help restore the quality of their surroundings.

I must say it was no surprise to me either that of all the threats—air and water pollution, the use of pesticides, the disappearance of open space, and the depletion of our wildlife—the public listed air pollution as the most pressing environmental problem confronting us today.

* * *

Dr. Robert Worth Frank begins an address "On Growing Old."

The circling year is bringing us nearer to the beginning of a new year and to another January first. Now the first of January cannot be treated with indifference. From it, men date their calendars, project their plans, and number their days. Furthermore, the end of an old year and the beginning of a new put one in a reflective mood about the passing of time. They remind us that we are all growing older, that some of us are growing old, and that others of us are so old that all we can do is to grow still older. So it is in order at this season of the year to think about growing old, and it is especially germane for an increasing number of us in our American society to reflect upon our personal problem of aging.

Were I to choose a text for such reflections, it would be from Psalm thirty-seven, verse twenty-five, the first half of the verse. The entire verse reads, "I have been young, and now am old; yet have I not seen the righteous forsaken, nor his seed begging bread." I shall let the second half of that verse rest in peace! For though it may have been true for the psalmist, it has not been altogether borne out in my experience. But the first half of that verse has come literally true for me (as it has for many others): "I have been young, and now am old." Let us think together about the meaning of this experience that comes to every one who lives long enough to be old.

Who are the old? We have no ready-made answer. We must acknowledge a certain relativity here. When the average lifespan was forty to fifty years, you were old at forty. The Pilgrim and Puritan fathers were old in their late twenties and early thirties. Today, the average life-duration is in the early seventies. So while chronological age is no sure sign of oldness (some are bent and slow, or disabled at sixty, others carry a full load at seventy-five or eighty), sixty-five is the magic line from which our society measures the start of old age. To soften the blow, the sociologists call sixty-five the youth of old age. My term for it is senior citizen, junior grade.

* * *

The former Colleen Moore, movie actress, begins an address.

Thank you very much, Mr. President, distinguished guests, and ladies and gentlemen.

About eight months ago, Doubleday published my book, "Silent Star," and since then I've been getting fan mail just like I used to do when I was a star.

Most of the fan mail asks me, "Wasn't it wonderful to live in Hollywood during the Twenties?"

It was. It was wonderful to be living in the Twenties, because in that very short, small period, this was a period of great creativity, and everyone was terribly young—not just in movies, but in all walks.

For example, in art, Chagall was under thirty; so was Modigliani; and Picasso was just under thirty.

In business Harley Earle, just out of art school, was designing the marvelous automobiles which made General Motors famous. He was twenty-eight. In Hollywood, everyone was very young, and almost everyone was under thirty. Irving Salzberg, who was the head of MGM, where they were making such wonderful pictures in that day, they call this little age, "The Golden Age"—Irving was twenty-eight. John McCormick, of the First National, twenty-seven; Julian Laemmle, of Universal, where they made all the great western pictures, Julian was twenty-five; Bailey Shulberg, who was the head of Paramount, I am sure was quite an old man because he must have been at least fifty; and in doing the research on my book I found he was an "old" thirty-two.

The reason that the actresses were so young was because of the camera. The camera in the early days was a very cruel and harsh thing; the lighting was bright and harsh; and only the youngest and finest skins could stand a closeup.

So, they took little teen-age girls and dressed them up as grown-up ladies; put up their hair; gave them high heels so they could have close-ups. A girl's career was all through by the time she was an "old hag" of twenty-one.

Then we heard that Lillian Gish, who was an "old hag" of twenty-one had made a picture called "Broken Blossoms," and in this picture she played a little, twenty-year-old girl, and looked twelve. We wondered what had happened. Mr. D. W. Griffith finally let out the secret. He had taken some black net, put it over the lens of the camera, and it acted as a retouching pencil, and Lillian, when the picture came out, looked not twelve, but ten. So, of course, then our careers were extended; and out of this came the diffusing lenses that made middle-aged actresses who shall be nameless, look like the great All-American Girl of today.

* * *

Mr. Stephen B. Labunski, President of NBC Radio Division begins an address.

Mr. President, Distinguished Guests, Gentlemen: I understand that our friend, Bob Lemon, went to the event which was graced by the presence of Vice President Humphrey last night. I won't ask him how it went, because it may spoil my story. The last time I heard Vice President Humphrey speak, he quoted his wife as saying to him before he left home, "Now remember, Hubert, to be memorable you don't have to be interminable."

* * *

Senator Robert Griffin of Michigan begins an address.

Thank you very much, President Wyatt, Senator Russell Arrington, Distinguished Guests, and Members of the Executives' Club of Chicago. The other day the Junior Senator from Illinois was introducing the Senior Senator from Illinois, and he said, "Everett Dirksen is probably the one person in the world who looks like he's been electrocuted but lived through it."

I'm glad to be here in this great forum, and to bring you the greetings of my two distinguished colleagues from Illinois who asked me to say hello to you for them.

Wyatt has made reference to the fact that I was something of an obstacle in President Johnson's path last year, and this prompts me to say that I wasn't always an obstacle.

I want to make that clear. There were occasions when I found it convenient, perhaps even magnanimous, to support President Johnson. For example, the nomination of Soapy Williams came up for him to be the Ambassador to the Philippines. I got up on the Senate floor, and gave a long speech about the qualifications, virtues, background and experience of Soapy Williams and indicated that I wanted my colleagues to support his nomination.

Then I said I hoped that no hidden meaning would be read into my words; that I wanted to wish Soapy a very active, fruitful, and LONG tour of duty on the other side of the world.

Well, actually, you know, despite our political differences, Soapy and I have been pretty good friends over the years, and in about a week I received a letter, and it said:

Dear Bob:

"I noticed in the papers, and I read in the Congressional Record, where you very generously supported my nomination to be Ambassador to the Philippines. I appreciate it very much. I hope you won't read any hidden meaning in my words but a great American served once in the Philippines and he said, 'I shall return.'"

Well, last week Soapy submitted his resignation to the President, and unless I can get President Nixon to refuse to accept it, he's going to be on his way back to Michigan.

Dwight D. Eisenhower begins an address to an audience of church women.

At the outset, I must express my appreciation of the honor I feel in speaking before this assemblage. An invitation to occupy this platform would confer distinction upon any man—perhaps I should say for any mere man—for you are gathered here in high purpose, inspired by an unshakable faith in yourselves, your country and your God.

I can hardly hope by my words to further your purpose or deepen your threefold faith.

That faith, immeasurable and imponderable, daily exemplified in millions of American families, is the prime strength of our great nation. It is the very basis of our society. And it is the most heartening support for those whose obligation is to represent you in the conduct of national, state and community affairs.

Though I cannot enhance the spiritual wealth that is yours, perhaps I can, by identifying some of the circumstances of today that emphasize the value of this faith, encourage you to spread its influence into every human activity in every community across our land.

Now, of course, the cynic—the Marxist, or the worshiper of machines and numbers—will scoff that faith is no armor against artillery, that the spirit weakens fast before the blast of the bomb. But your husbands and brothers and fathers can testify that, in the terrifying nakedness of the battlefield, the faith and the spirit of men are the keys of survival and victory.

Faith is evidently too simple a thing for some to recognize in its paramount worth. Yet the present and the future demand men and women who are firm in their faith in our country and unswerving in their service to her. This is true in every basic unit of our political and social life—in the family, the community, the state and the nation.

* * *

Dr. John A. Howard, Rockford College, begins a commencement address at The Radford School, El Paso, Texas.

My role this evening is to try to penetrate the post-exam exhaustion and the excitement and sadness you may feel, and try to say something sufficiently inspirational and helpful to register as a fitting culmination to your schoolwork here.

On a similar occasion, Bob Hope made a comment which that audience won't forget. He remarked it was customary at Commencement to offer some advice to the seniors as they move into the grim conditions of the real world. "My advice as you move out into the real world," he said, "can be phrased very briefly. Don't go!"

As one surveys the real world today, it almost seems as if there is more wisdom than wit in his comment. The Vietnam war continues to be a profound concern. The Israeli-Arab antagonism goes on boiling. The population boom threatens to be even more troublesome than military strife if peace could ever be secured. Crime, violence, revolution and anarchy are increasing in the affluent nations. Government spending seems to be completely out of hand. And the caterpillar, which our youngest daughter so triumphantly found, died before it made a cocoon.

Things don't look so good!

Well, if you have an inclination to think your generation has more than its share of unfavorable circumstances, and if you tend to feel sorry for yourself, forget it. Think back through history and you will recognize that man has never had an easy time of it, and more often than not has lived under the threat of some very great peril.

The Black Death wiped out a quarter of the population of Europe in the 1300s. The potato crop failure in Ireland in 1845 and 1846 literally eliminated the principal source of food for a nation. Through most of Western history, one powerful tyrant or another was trying to capture the civilized world. Contemplate the development of our own country—the first meager settlements scratched out of a wilderness, the continuing battles with the British and French and Indians for each new bit of territory. If you remember that in the three days of the

Battle of Gettysburg, there were 53,000 casualties, even the Vietnam war takes on a rather different perspective.

The point is this. Life is not easy, and it is only recently that man has become naive enough or comfortable enough to think it should be. The measure of your own satisfaction and fulfillment during your years will not be the degree of protection and ease which happens to be granted to you, but the choices you make and the things which you create. Viktor Frankl states the point magnificently when he asserts that man's greatest freedom is the freedom to choose how he will respond to his circumstances.

* * *

Mr. William I. Nichols, Editor and Publisher of This Week Magazine, used a quotation effectively in opening an address.

Thank you for a very kind introduction.

I always think of your friend, and mine, Adlai Stevenson, who once opened up by saying, "I never mind a little praise just so long as it is fulsome."

* * *

Mr. Jerris J. Babb begins an address.

I understand that a few years ago a gentleman by the name of Alexander Wolcott had the privilege of addressing a luncheon meeting of a very large women's organization in Washington, and while he was being introduced to the thousand or so ladies assembled, his stomach started to rumble, and pretty soon he came forth with a very audible burp. The lady who was introducing him turned around and glared at him. He shrugged his shoulders and said, "Well, lady, what did you expect—chimes?"

* * *

John N. Mitchell, Attorney General of the United States, begins an address.

You and I must not take comfort in the historic palliative that crime is an old phenomenon. It is true that crime has always afflicted human society. It is always true that all civilized societies have dedicated their resources to control crime—to establish and maintain a code of conduct to serve the needs of the people.

The American public must not be mollified by recollection of the past as in San Francisco 100 years ago when—and I quote from a journal of the period—"No decent man was in safety to walk the street after dark, while at all hours both day and night, his property was jeopardized by incendiarism and burglary."

In this nation, we continue to combat crime drawing on the philosophies of the great common lawyers of the 17th and 18th centuries—on Coke and Blackstone—and on the enlightenment principles of Jefferson and the Framers of our Constitution.

The goal of our nation is freedom and personal dignity for all our citizens. And we have yet to prove to the world that, in the long run, this constitutional experiment will endure.

Today, crime has assumed a new and frightening dimension which is casting in doubt our traditional ability to be the free and independent men that our forefathers were.

The simple fact is that crime is intimidating us—is forcing us—to change the fabric of our society and our inability to control crime is a courtship with national disaster.

* * *

Dr. John S. Gibson begins an address.

My basic proposition is that a revolution in citizenship education in America's high schools is desperately needed if these schools are to continue to serve as the principal public agents by transmitting and strengthening the values of our democratic society to the young people of today and tomorrow. My central recommendation is that viable and significant links be established between the processes of education related to the school and the life and environment of students in order to advance young people toward specific and desirable behaviors fundamental to the democratic civic culture. My main problem is that of redundancy of pleas, but my shining hope is an optimism that, together, we can recognize the challenges facing us and can join forces in translating those challenges into effective action.

* * *

Arthur E. Meyerhoff begins an address.

I am one of those people that sociologists, political scientists, educators, novelists and others have referred to during the past 20 years as "hucksters," "men in gray flannel suits," "Madison Avenue Boys," and "Hidden Persuaders."

No, we haven't been exactly spoiled by flattery. The late Bernard DeVoto referred to advertising as "a cult, a system of shamans." Arthur Schlesinger, Jr. offered us the cheerful news that our work "has been successful in retarding the arts, tarnishing the virtues, and confusing the manners of our country."

Advertising is nothing more than the arts of persuasion practiced in mass media.

And persuasion is practiced in almost every human endeavor—the doctor with a good bedside manner, the professor whose classes are crowded, and the baby with a sweet smile. But it is the skilled people in advertising who practice persuasion in depth scientifically.

* * *

Eugene H. Methvin, Associate Editor of The Reader's Digest, begins an address.

In 1776 news of the signing of the Declaration of Independence required a month to travel from Philadelphia to Savannah, a distance of 750 miles. Last March a woman in College Park, Georgia, watching a television newscast saw a young soldier in Vietnam cut down by a Viet Cong bullet. In horror she realized the soldier was her own son. The next day, indeed, an Army official came to confirm what she had seen: Her son had been killed in action 10,000 miles away.

Thus technology has magnified explosively the speed and power American journalists can command. And this power is a little frightening. Today as never before people within and without the ranks of the Fourth Estate are questioning profoundly what journalists do and why. The old canons seem no longer valid. There simply are no guidelines, no body of experience, journalists can draw on in charting their way today.

For today's situation is absolutely unprecedented in the history of human civilization. Man has been in existence perhaps 2½ million years. But he did not start living in permanent settlements until as recently as the Neolithic Age, some 10,000 years ago. There were no cities as large as 100,000 human beings until as recently as Greco-Roman civilization, only 2500 years ago. And no city reached a million until London hit the mark about 1830. By 1900 only ten cities in the world had that many people. Today 133 do, and seven have over ten million. And all are linked by instantaneous communication.

* * *

Roger Hull begins an introduction.

I have always believed that any institution's greatest assets are its human assets . . . for work is accomplished by people, not by methods or machines or systems.

It is clear that the Newcomen Society shares this belief because it has been the practice to honor both institutions and individuals.

I am grateful for the opportunity to introduce Maxey Jarman and Ben Willingham of GENESCO, Inc.

* * *

Frederic J. Robbins begins an address describing the company of which he is the head.

The price of butter had just soared to twenty-seven cents a pound and milk reached a new high of seven cents a quart; the annual income was $486 per worker; the nation's population had exploded to almost sixty-three million, and a fellow by the name of James Naismith devised a new game called basketball. The year was 1891—the same year Colonel S. E. Bliss and John E. Laughlin decided to form a partnership and open a shafting works in Harvey, Illinois, a new town on the outskirts of Chicago.

A comparison of these bits of nostalgia with current supermarket prices, wage and population statistics, and the seven-foot athletes darting across our television screens illustrates one of the most basic of historic axioms—there is nothing so permanent as change. Bliss & Laughlin has changed dramatically since its formation almost eighty years ago, and it seems to me that our successful history to this point must be attributed to this constant adaptation to change. The history of Bliss & Laughlin, and, correspondingly, its success, illustrate the inherent pragmatism of industrial development in this country —taking existing problems and situations and turning them into corporate advantages.

* * *

Lieutenant General Donald L. Putt begins an address at the Polytechnic Institute of Brooklyn.

It is a great privilege to be here tonight with such a distinguished group. I am most grateful for the honor that Brooklyn Polytechnic will confer on me Wednesday evening and I shall accept that honor with deep humility and a sense of great responsibility.

Years ago I read that "a good executive was one who decided to do the impossible and then hired some bright young men to carry out his decisions." Without making any claims for being a good executive, I do want to acknowledge the great assistance of those bright young men and associates without whose help I am sure you would not be honoring me here tonight.

* * *

The Most Reverend John J. Wright begins a Commencement address at the University of Notre Dame.

"Behold how they are numbered among the children of God, and their lot is among the saints!"

Our sermon this day can well be brief. It is a commonplace to remind college graduates that they are a privileged group. Nevertheless, I ask you to meditate on your privileges for just a moment. You men of Notre Dame are privileged in more ways than you may usually recall. You were privileged in the circumstances of your birth. It is a very real privilege to be born in America, to be born under the physical and spiritual, the civil and religious conditions which normally prevail in the parts of the United States from which most of you are privileged to come. Despite the moods of discouragement and disillusion which occasionally prevail among us, it is a very real privilege to have been born in this particular period of history, face to face alike with the opportunity for the alert and the challenge to the valiant which always exist in a time like the present, a time of revolution and far-reaching changes.

Most of you, I trust all of you are privileged in the families from which you come. Our typical college students come from frugal, hard-working people. In the main they do not come from the background of that poverty which degrades nor of the wealth which degenerates. Thanks to the industry of our people and to the relatively equal opportunities of our land, our typical families tend at the moment to be moderately prosperous.

* * *

Judge John A. Matthews begins an address dedicating a new high school building.

This is an auspicious and purposeful occasion. We have witnessed the dedication of a new high school building, within the hallowed halls and classrooms of which, young men will receive intellectual and moral education and training to make them, not only good citizens of our beloved Nation, but also citizens of the city of God.

* * *

John Foster Dulles as Secretary of State begins an address.

Anniversaries can be both pleasant and useful occasions. This meeting is of that kind. We look backward and see much that was good. We look forward and see much promise.

The United Nations has already shown that it is here to stay. One proof is the presence here of 37 foreign ministers who have come from all parts of the earth. Another proof is the fact that, since its founding, no member nation has sought to withdraw; and there is a long, too long, waiting list of qualified nations which want to become members.

This esteem for the United Nations is based on solid accomplishments.

* * *

Sheldon S. Cohen begins an address as U. S. Commissioner of Internal Revenue.

I hadn't thought—it is hard for a tax collector to think of funny stories with which to start talks, but maybe it is appropriate for this day that Matthew was a tax collector until he got religion. Maybe we can give some people religion today. I have often told the rabbi at my synagogue that I suspect we give more people religion than all the ministers in the country.

I would like to talk to you today about some rather modern, advanced concepts in the administration of what is perhaps the most complex, most successful revenue system ever devised.

* * *

John T. Connor opens an address in Chicago.

If anybody wants to see America in action, this is where the action is.

This is America, right here, in all its wonderful and dazzling diversity. The driving forces of the American dream are nowhere more evident.

Of course, you can never really catch up with a dream, at least never really. But the grander it is, the harder you try— which is why Chicago and the Nation are always going to be on the move, always straining against the harness of possibility —always in the lead.

Industry seems to never rest here, and you can almost sense the surging of Chicago's tremendous energy, striving, as it always has, as it always will, to forge the future in the shape of its dream; and to make it good enough and prosperous enough to fulfill everyone's hopes and satisfy everyone's needs.

But the roster of your membership, and the scope of operations of the companies you represent, indicate that, for all the advantages of your home base, your interests lie far beyond the reaches of this city, of this state, and of this region. And this is as it should and must be in an economy as interdependent and interrelated such as ours today.

No region is insulated against, or isolated from the other any more. All are intimately linked because all are integral to the functioning of the national economy, and all are affected by it.

* * *

Louis B. Lundborg, Chairman, Bank of America, opens an address.

Just last week I heard the Governor of the State of Montana tell about two old friends of his that were discussing something a little bit related to what I am going to talk about here this noon. They were gentlemen of quite separate branches of the Christian faith and the two have often been at odds with each other over theology. But in spite of that, they had become very close friends.

One day recently, one of them said to the other, "Isn't it a wonderful thing that we could become such good friends that we could even talk about our religious differences?"

"Yes, this is nice. I don't see any reason why we can't go right on doing this. I don't see any reason why we can't go right on pursuing our various and respective missions in life. You will do the Lord's work in your way and I will do it in His."

B. CLOSING A SPEECH

All that I say to you rests upon one truth which I firmly believe. I tried to speak it on the day when I took my oath of office as President of the United States. The truth is:

"Whatever America hopes to bring to pass in the world must first come to pass in the heart of America."

I know no more plain or pure ideal to which we can pledge our lives.

I know of no other way we can prove worthy of freedom.
—*Dwight D. Eisenhower closes an address*

I most firmly believe that the American people's decision to strengthen our country in moral leadership, in intellectual stature, in military posture, in a dependable prosperity widely shared will be realized. Underlying that decision is a tremendous spiritual energy which I believe to be adequate to every test. I believe that it grows from day to day as our people become more and more aware of the deadly nature of the world's struggle.

I most firmly believe, too, that world leadership in the cause of cooperative peace lies within the capacity of America. This capacity will be realized when everyone here present uses his mind and his will and all his resources in union with others of like influence to bring about the understanding, the comprehension, the determination we need. Freedom of expression is not merely a right—in the circumstances of today, its constructive use is a stern duty. Have we, have you as publishers, the courage fully to exercise the right and perform the duty?

Along with patriotism, understanding, comprehension, determination are the qualities we now need. Without them we cannot win. With them we cannot fail.—*Dwight D. Eisenhower*

* * *

The hope of the free world in the ultimate triumph of international economic cooperation lies in the men of good will, who believe that:

> In Christ there is no East or West,
> In Him no South or North;
> But one great fellowship of love
> Throughout the whole wide earth.

In our action against misery, hunger and despair we have to dedicate ourselves to God and to have in our hearts the Apostles' Creed: "We believe in the kingdom of God as the divine rule in human society; and in the brotherhood of man under the Fatherhood of God."—*Professor Andrew Rockover-Cecil, McMurry College*

But let me leave you with one final thought: Crime is deep-rooted and ugly and its defeat will take many years of hard work. If your volunteer project is with juvenile delinquents, be prepared to face rejection. If your project is prisons, be prepared to face despondency and failure—symbols of the urban crisis. Be prepared to face poverty and ignorance, human misery and obscenities. Be prepared to endure and to fight long and hard.—*John N. Mitchell closes an address*

* * *

While reminding you of your obligations to Democracy, I make an appeal this morning for the development among you of a spiritual aristocracy, an elite of mind and heart and soul. You will do this best by frequently meditating on your privileges and by recognizing effectively the responsibilities which arise from them. Even as the correlative of right is duty, so that of privilege is responsibility. Duties correspond to the rights of others; responsibilities are attached to something in ourselves, our offices, our own dignities, our talents, our positions, our privileges. Your privileges obligate you to the sources whence they came, to the families that gave you temporal advantages; to the Church that gave you baptism, your re-birth to life everlasting; to the University which in so many ways acts for all these as the guardian of your privileges and the guide to the responsibilities correlative to them.—*The Most Reverend John J. Wright closes a commencement address at the University of Notre Dame*

C. CHAIRMAN'S COMMENTS AFTER THE SPEECH

Thank you Ambassador Linowitz for an instructive address on the major aspects of foreign policy in this hemisphere. We are indebted to you for it.

* * *

Mr. Ambassador (Charles E. Bohlen), we are indebted to you for a frank and excellent presentation of a subject of major importance to all of us.

Thank you for a thoughtful and stimulating analysis of the issues and problems we need to consider for a better understanding of Latin America.

* * *

We are greatly indebted to you, Senator Percy, for this frank analysis of some extremely complex and difficult international problems.

* * *

Governor, the response of the audience speaks for itself. We're delighted to have you with us.

* * *

We thank you for your thoughtful message. We have time now for a few questions.

* * *

Mr. Bartlett, you have been a wonderful speaker. We have enjoyed having you. Thank you very, very much.

The meeting is adjourned.

* * *

In closing I do want to say that I believe there is an acceleration of interest and increasing participation on the part of industry in this matter of bringing about the peacetime use of the atom.

We have not time for questions today, and so it is with the hope that our three speakers have been able to bring you a better understanding of some of the problems of atomic energy that we close our meeting. Thank you very much.—*Walter L. Cisler*

* * *

Dr. Appel, I speak for everyone here when I express our gratitude to you for sharing with us your responsible view regarding the future of medicine. It is encouraging to each of us to know that such men as yourself are working with the government to direct the medical bills before Congress and the Medicare program.

Thank you very much, Mr. Watson, for that very interesting address. We have a number of questions here.

* * *

Miss Adams, we are deeply indebted to you for your thoughtful comments, and I have many more questions than you are going to be able to provide the time to answer. But let me pick them at random.